Teaching
as a
Conserving
Activity

*Books by Neil Postman
and Charles Weingartner*

TEACHING AS A SUBVERSIVE ACTIVITY
THE SOFT REVOLUTION
LINGUISTICS
THE SCHOOL BOOK

by Neil Postman

CRAZY TALK, STUPID TALK

Teaching as a Conserving Activity

by
Neil Postman

DELACORTE PRESS/NEW YORK

Published by
Delacorte Press
1 Dag Hammarskjold Plaza
New York, New York 10017
A portion of this book first appeared in *Atlantic Monthly*.

Manufactured in the United States of America

First printing

Designed by Laura Bernay

Library of Congress Cataloging in Publication Data

Postman, Neil.
    Teaching as a conserving activity.

    1. Education—Philosophy. 2. Postman, Neil.
3. Mass media and children. 4. Children—Language.
5. Audio-visual education. 6. Curriculum planning.
I. Title.
LB885.P65T4   371.1'02   79–10728
ISBN 0–440–08651–5

Contents

Prologue

During the past twelve years Charles Weingartner and I have written five books together. Each book put forward ideas which seemed important to us but not at any time unassailable. Our awareness of our own deficiencies, as well as the elusiveness of our subjects, shielded us from falling in love with what we had written. In fact, as we were building our arguments, we were at all times accompanied by the claims of legitimate counterarguments. For every idea we expressed as "true," we could easily think of its opposite, or at least of some alternative, as also true. It was as if we and our shadow were looking at the matter from opposite poles; our right was his left, his right our left. We understood which way we were facing but it was not hard for us to imagine others, or even ourselves, facing in another direction. As a consequence of this double vision, Charlie suggested early in our collaboration that the last sentence of each of our books should be "Or vice versa."

The idea struck me then, as it does still, as paradoxical. To conclude a bookful of intense argument with the sentence "Or vice versa" is, in fact, a very serious thing to do, which is to say, it is a joke; which is to say further, it shows a proper respect for your own limitations. But at the same time readers are likely to think you have trivialized your own work and led them down a primrose path. Earnestness, it would seem, is the enduring mark of a serious person. It is also, as Russell Baker has said, man's oldest con game. But the fact is that there are simply too many people who think that humor and seriousness are opposites. And so we decided not to end our books with "Or vice versa."

The Earth has gone around the sun twelve times since the publication of our best-known book, *Teaching as a Subversive Activity*. I do not seem to be facing in the same direction as I was in 1967. Frankly, I do not know if I have turned or everything else has. But many of the arguments which then seemed merely opposite, now seem acutely apposite, and this book is the result of a change in perspective. It is the vice versa of that earlier book. That is, it is my vice versa. I do this one alone, as you will have noticed. But I suspect Charlie Weingartner will know how serious an undertaking it is. And I trust you will, as well.

Introduction

Sometime in 1971 an education conference was held at Fordham University in the Bronx. The Konference (spelled with a *k,* as a petulant expression of rebellion) was mainly for "radical critics" who were in need of gathering in order to share their old grievances and to collect some fresh ones. As it happened, some months earlier *The New York Times Magazine* had published an article in which I had been identified as a "leading education radical." This was a mistake, from my point of view, on the order of naming Terence, Cardinal Cooke as a leading exponent of birth control. But radicals are no less susceptible to believing in the infallibility of *The New York Times* than the rest of us, and in due course I was invited to display my ideas at the Fordham conference. Why I accepted the invitation is another story. But having no radical ideas to put forward, I spent the thirty minutes allotted me describing an unusual high school program I had helped to develop in New Rochelle, New York. Halfway through, I became aware that the audience was less than pleased with what it was hearing—let us say, in the same way you might be displeased if after putting on a Frank Sinatra record at a particularly romantic moment, you heard him giving a lecture on the evils of smoking. Among other things, it sort of spoils the mood.

As a result, the audience turned surly, and when I was done, the question period took the form of a bombardment of insult. The gist of it all was that I lacked nerve, guts, brains, and most of all, an understanding of the profound corruption of the "Amerikan" way of life (you could *hear* it being pronounced with a *k*). This way of life, I was told, could not be set aright by some niggling changes in a high school curriculum. As if to show me the way, a young man put forward the following imagery, punctuated at the end by a fiercely-asked question: The USS *Wasp* lay in port at Fifty-seventh Street, its decks heavy with fighter aircraft and other implements of destruction. Its destination, Viet Nam. To an education critic, he said, there was no other response to this opportunity than to blow the *Wasp* clear out of the water. The question followed inexorably, Would I be willing to help him do it? (Excited applause.)

The logistics of blowing up the USS *Wasp* were no more intriguing to me than was the logic behind the proposal: You cannot improve a classroom until you have improved a school. But you cannot improve a school until you have improved a community, and you cannot improve a community until you have improved the society from which it derives its values. Thus, the serious education critic begins his work topside, so to speak, by attacking the military-industrial complex. Frankly, I did not disagree that America could be improved, in some abstract sense, by the elimination of the USS *Wasp,* although it seemed pretty clear to me that an education critic who began his work with that project would also end it on the same project.

I do not remember exactly what I said in response to the question, but I do remember thinking that this must be the beginning of the end of the education reform movement. The young people gathered in that room were among the best that America was producing—serious, caring, sensitive. Many were college students or graduates. Most had read the literature of the reform movement. All were primed to give their energies to a humane cause. Yet, somehow, it had come to this. How to improve education? Blow up the USS *Wasp!*

I was right, sad to say. Later that year Ivan Illich's *Deschooling Society* appeared, signifying the end of the school reform movement. Illich had merely concluded that the schools were not reformable and that the best path to the future lay in eliminating them altogether. This proposal, of course, was the thinking man's equivalent of blowing up the USS *Wasp;* that is to say, it proposed nothing. Disguising itself as hardheaded social comment, the book was a celebration of impotence, and soon thereafter Illich turned his attention to the hypothetical elimination of other social institutions. But his book did provoke the question, as it does still, How is it that the education reform movement, which began with such a firm hold on the facts, ended in such ridiculous flights of fantasy?

The essential facts of American education are as obvious as they are immovable. There are approximately forty-five million students attending more than ninety thousand schools, under the supervision of roughly two million teachers, at a cost, each year, in excess of eighty billion dollars. To change what the students and teachers do to each other, or how and where they do it, would require sustained and rigorous criticism, accompanied by the invention of multiple alternatives of a practical nature. The literature of the reform movement of the sixties had set out to do just that. For example, John Holt's honorable and extraordinary little book, *How Children Fail.* Written in the form of a diary, covering a period from 1958 to 1961, the book was a description of the behavior and feelings of elementary school students as they tried to cope with the demands of typical

American classrooms. In his account Holt invented nothing and discovered nothing. But like all important social commentators, he made us remember what we all once knew but had chosen to forget: in this instance, that the experience of school is characterized by boredom, confusion, and fear. Especially fear. Fear of not having the right answer, fear of not understanding things the way everyone else does, fear of being singled out, fear of not being singled out, fear of reproach, of ridicule, of failure. For many children the school is a House of Fear, no matter how charming its architecture, or open its halls, or contemporary its materials.

As his later books have shown, Holt is no educational philosopher; he does not have an intelligible set of principles on which to base a program of change. But he knows, or at least once knew, a wound when he sees one. And his book was a catalogue of damages inflicted by a typical middle-class system of schooling. For thousands of readers, one imagines, *How Children Fail* rekindled remembrances of wounds past, and from their number came dozens of articulate men and women to write angry tracts about this or that part of the education system.

These writers were not philosophers of education, either. Among them there were no Deweys, or Kilpatricks, or Counts, or Ruggs, or Hooks. No ideology bound them. No plan for social reconstruction. Not even a clear vision of the future. They were—how shall I say it?—ad hoc critics. Teachers, journalists, psychologists, playwrights, parents, who, like Holt, knew a wound when they saw one, and demanded that a stop be put to what they construed as intellectual and emotional carnage. I have not verified it but having known many of these critics, I am willing to bet that nine out of ten of them had hated school. It was "getting even" time, and they spoke not only for the children they once were but for the children who were being forced to relive their experience.

Whatever else their shortcomings, these were tough, reality-oriented critics, at least at the beginning. Herb Kohl *(36 Children)*, Jonathan Kozol *(Death at an Early Age)*, Nat Hentoff *(Our Children Are Dying)*, James Herndon *(The Way It Spozed to Be)*, George Dennison *(The Lives of Children)*—their point of entry was the real-life experience of children in school, and their criticisms were aimed at specific procedures and policies that made school (as Charles Silberman called it) a "mindless" place. They ripped into the curriculum, the regimentation, the industrial mentality, the grading system, standardized tests, school bureaucracy, homogeneous grouping, and all the other assumptions and conventions which gave the classroom (and still do) its peculiar character.

Some of them got so far as to propose alternatives, although in this they were not gifted, and were, one might say, even a bit ridiculous. The "free school" movement, which became the center of interest for a while, clearly offered no relief to the millions of children attending public schools, and the scores of "alternative schools" that sprung up did not always give realistic hints as to how public education might improve itself.

And then suddenly, it was over. Like a summer cloudburst that catches everyone unawares, does its sound and fury, and leaves no trace of itself. In this case, with not even a rainbow left behind; only a dull, leaden sky. The situation had not been much improved or even very much clarified. Everything, as of today, looks quite the same as before.

What happened? Where did all the critics go? And their movement? And all their angry, spirited defenses of the oppressed? The history of that time has yet to be written, and when it is, it must be done by someone more objective than the likes of me. But I can make some guesses about what happened, and if I am right, there may be a lesson or two to be learned—for next time around.

First, the Viet Nam War ended. More than we suspected, the energy and fury of the education reform movement was a spillover from the antiwar movement. The young man who wanted to blow up the USS *Wasp* was, so to speak, only an education radical for the day. And by deflection. He and many others like him had turned in bitterness toward education because the American war machine seemed so much more impervious to reform than the schools. It is easier, they thought, to change the destination of a school than an aircraft carrier. They were wrong, of course, but the point is that what they hated was not the "mindlessness" of the schools but the mindlessness of the war. When that ended, so did their interest in education. The wellspring of their resentment went dry.

Second, among those who were genuinely interested in the schools, there was an insufficient understanding of the complexity of the school as a social institution. In reading the early John Holt, for example, one gets the impression that if only teachers could be made to grasp how children fail, classrooms would change their character almost at once. But, of course, a school has a multifaceted agenda and many constituents to serve. Parents, publishers, politicans, labor unions, state requirements, administrative convenience— each makes its demands and exacts its price. The classroom is not a place of simple teacher-student interaction—not even when the teacher closes the door. It is a place in which the claims of various political, social, and economic interests are negotiated. The classroom is both a symbol and a product of deadly serious cultural bargaining. Everyone gets a say in its business, including Anita Bryant. Charles Silberman couldn't have been more wrong in calling the classroom "mindless." The classroom reflects with considerable precision the workings of many minds. One suspects that as the ambiguities implicit in this fact became apparent, many school critics were overwhelmed and turned to other seemingly less intractable matters such as the children's rights movement and nonschool learning environments.

Third, some of the critics were, to put it in nonpsychiatric terms, utopians. They were not satisfied, for very long, to redress a grievance or improve a procedure or eliminate a bit of nonsense. They sought total change. Illich reflects this fatal defect most clearly but other less well-known critics were also plagued by it. The trouble with being a utopian, of course, is that it is a form of self-flagellation and is likely to leave one distraught or cranky or devoid of all interest in the subject. None of that is very helpful to children, still less to utopian critics themselves, some of whom retired to mountains, spas, communes, and other places of spiritual intensity, where their utopias could exist in the only place utopias can exist—in the imagination.

Fourth, many critics had a well-developed contempt for teachers and administrators, the very people who would have to carry through the proposed reforms. Oddly, many of the critics were teachers themselves but not a few suffered from the "Nobody understands but me" complex. In any case, with few exceptions (Herb Kohl, for one) school critics did not even try to provide teachers with materials and methods that would reflect significant education change. The widespread belief was that "establishment" teachers would probably defile the new ideas and that administrators were beyond redemption. Thus, some critics, burdened by a crippling self-righteousness, cut themselves off from their most influential constituency, the adults who run the schools.

At the same time, the student population was viewed as through a Rousseauian glass, unrealistically. Typically a school was imagined to be a place of obtuse, malignant adults who were dedicated to oppressing pure-hearted, liberty-seeking, instinctively humane children. With such cartoon imagery as this, it is no wonder so little was accomplished and that it ended so soon.

Fifth, there were too few critics who had any official connection with schools of education, state departments of education, or other similar agencies from which their ideas could be fed into the classroom. Some did have such connections but most did not, which meant, among other things, that they could not *make a living* as education critics. This, in turn, meant that many of the best critics had to repair fairly quickly to their natural sources of income and interest. It also meant that the official routes of influence remained relatively untouched by new ideas.

Sixth, concomitant with the emergence of the school reform movement there arose what may be charitably described as the Age of Self-Improvement, which Age continues with seemingly inexhaustible energy to the present time. In the modern sense, improving yourself requires getting in touch with your feelings, shedding layers of inhibition, exorcising guilt, never saying yes when you mean no, doing your own thing, and, in general, minimizing such demands of civilization as may intrude themselves on your heightened consciousness. For the most part the well-known critics did not suffer from this disorder. But many younger people who, at first, were their natural allies and connection with the future did, and they soon withdrew in large numbers from the social arena to tend the windmills of their own minds. The consequences for school reform were severe since social action and navel-watching do not go well together. Without a high-energy, well-focused cadre of young people to carry forward their ideas, school critics were disarmed and much of their mission disabled.

Finally, and almost too obvious to mention, there was the much publicized and deeply felt decline in the economic situation, which led to education cutbacks and frozen staffs. It is a principle universally to be observed that when people are worried about getting or holding jobs, they do not make first-rate social critics. It may also be observed that as the more intelligent young people sought livelihoods in professions other than education, there were (and are) fewer "young Turks" to carry forward the critical tradition.

What of the future? For the moment, serious school criticism is barely alive, except for what is called the "back to the basics" movement. A lecture on seventeenth-century Venetian glassblowing can draw as large a crowd as a lecture on the school curriculum. A lecture on improving your backhand, twice the crowd. A lecture on astrology, ten times. But it is well to remember that school criticism is seasonal work. There is an ebb and flow to the public's interest in education, and I believe the phrase for where we are now is neap tide. But a concern for how education is done, like the tides, never goes away entirely, not here in America. The reason is that our experiment in public education is probably the most important contribution we have so far made to world civilization. In America, as Lawrence Cremin once wisely observed, whenever we need a revolution, we get a new curriculum; which is to say, more than we acknowledge, our public schools lie at the center of our own civilization. When the tide shifts, as in the course of things it must, there will be another crest of criticism. And perhaps we will have learned something from the last wave.

In any case, this is the context in which the present book appears. I do not expect that it will release new and vast energies devoted to serious school criticism, although if it should, nothing would please me more. I find it hard to bear that the field has been left to "back to the basics" advocates. There is so much more that needs to be said than can be encompassed in that baleful philosophy. Yet I must hasten to add that I have not attempted to encompass so much in my own. There are interesting and complex issues about school—busing, taxes, children's rights, teachers' unions, school boards, to name a few—on which I have nothing to say. I have chosen to speak, naturally, on that which I judge to be the most important issue: What should be taught in school?—no matter how children get there, or how many there are, or what their color may be, or how much their teachers are paid.

Accordingly, the book is divided into three sections. The first consists of one chapter in which, as economically as possible, I have stated the general principle on which decisions about what should be taught ought to be made. The second section consists of five chapters wherein I attempt to state the major problems which our teaching must respond to. The final section, consisting of six chapters, offers proposals for how we might proceed.

Perhaps it is a mere conceit but I believe that the proposals in Section III will not be entirely comprehensible unless you have read the statement of the problems in Section II, which, in turn, will not make sense unless you have first understood the principle on which the whole book rests. In other words, the book is conceived as an argument, with a beginning, middle, and an end. It is not the most detailed argument I could have provided. I think of my proposals, for example, as a blueprint, not an edifice. But I have tried to make my argument clear, and I should be very interested to know what are its refutations, for that is how conversation begins. Perhaps we do not require a new "movement" after all. Only a good conversation.

The
Perspective

1
The Thermostatic View

There is a group of aborigines in western Australia that has survived more or less intact for over twenty thousand years. Although they do not think of themselves as having an education philosophy, we can guess that they have one and that it is very good indeed. It has produced the kind of people needed to live effectively within the conditions of their culture, which is exactly what an education philosophy is supposed to do. In twenty thousand years there has never been a need for innovations, or alternatives, or new directions, or even moving back to the basics. That is, not until now. In having the bad luck to come to our recent notice, these people will soon enough be confronted with the biases of our own civilization; first through the intrusion of our anthropologists in search of PhD's, then through our bulldozers in search of materials, and finally through our media in search of audiences. Their twenty-thousand-year-old culture will come apart, and their twenty-thousand-year-old curriculum will be of no use since skill in spearhunting tends to be irrelevant to one's survival on a freeway.

Still, twenty thousand years is a long run for an education

philosophy. It merits our respect not only for its awesome durability but because in all that time not one textbook was required to explain it nor one education conference to promote it. Its unmodified, continuous usefulness was made possible of course by the fact that very little change took place in the society it served. That was the key. In such a society an education philosophy gets worked out early, and once for all, and then may be ignored in favor of more compelling matters; that is, it becomes invisible.

In our own society no such longterm lease can or ought to be granted to an education philosophy. Too many things are moving—are always moving—to be accommodated by a fixed point of view. Too many different things need to be done, and then undone, by education as the conditions of living change. In a society such as ours, there is something profoundly wrong in one's "holding" an education philosophy. Unless one can get rid of it as conditions require. Education is a culture's answer to the questions of a particular era. The hazard of "holding" an education philosophy is that you may be caught with a bag full of right answers to the wrong era. In holding a philosophy, one is held by it as well. There is something about a philosophy that can get one's ankles encased in concrete so that it is quite impossible to take another position.

What is wanted, as E. M. Forster once remarked, is inconsistency without frivolity. In other words, some philosophical mobility. Especially now. The same bulldozers, freeways, and media that attack an unsuspecting aborigine culture attack our own as well, and the question arises, Can we find a philosophy which will defend us against the assault of change?

This, of course, is a question the aborigines must ask, too. How they will handle it, I do not know and cannot even imagine. They are not accustomed to asking, let alone answering, such a question, and they do not have available a repertoire of education philosophies from which they may find and choose an appropriate path. Neither do they have the experience or training to analyze the nature of the changes occurring, which is a necessary preparation for knowing how and what to choose. All in all, it does not look good for the aborigines.

For us, things look a little better. At least in theory. We have had to ask this question many times before. We have available a variety of philosophies from which to find an answer, and we are accustomed to arguing, this way and that, about their merit. We know something, though not enough, about the nature of the changes we have inflicted upon ourselves. And alongside of all this, we have a principle which may serve as a guide in helping us to find satisfactory solutions, through education, to the threats of accelerating change.

I refer to the principle implied in the word *balance.* It is the same principle implied by the word *homeostasis.* The Greeks expressed it in the phrase "All things in moderation," and they also gave us the word, *oikos,* from which the most recent and forceful expression of the principle has surfaced: ecology. Modern biologists and zoologists have appropriated the word and the ideas embedded in it—to their great intellectual benefit and to the equally great deficit of the rest of us. Their exclusive franchise can and should be revoked at the earliest opportunity. For ecology is not essentially about DDT, caterpillars, and the effects on muskrats of diverting a stream. Ecology is about the rate and scale and structure of change within an environment. It is about how balance is achieved, a balanced mind and society as well as a balanced forest. It is, therefore, as much about social institutions, bulldozers, freeways, artifacts, and ideas as it is about natural processes, trees, rivers, and the survival of herons. As a matter of fact, the Greek word from which "ecology" is derived does not direct our attention to the natural environment at all. We first come across it meaning *house* or *household,* and Aristotle's use of the word is in political terms: The stability of one's household is weakened as the state increasingly intervenes in social affairs.

But leaving etymology aside, the field of education, as well as any other, must have full access to the enduring principle associated with the idea of ecology. Armed with this principle, we have an approach to understanding and addressing the problematic relationship between education and culture change. Simply stated, the principle is this: The stability and vitality of an environment depend not on what is *in* the environment but on the interplay of its elements; that is, on their diverse and dynamic complementarities. Exactly how things complement each other is a vast and difficult subject— is, in fact, the subject matter of ecology—but without doubt the most important form of complementarity is opposition.

From an ecological point of view, nothing is good in itself. For every yin, so to speak, there must be a yang. What makes something good or useful is the existence of some opposing force which keeps it under control. Is cellular growth "good" in a human organism? The question is meaningless. The regeneration and growth of human cells is good only when there are chemical reactions which retard its profligacy. Without them we die of cancer. Is the development of individual autonomy desirable? Only to the extent that it is modulated by the constraints of social norms. Is the exercise of political power good? Only where there exist opposing forces to hold it in check. There is no change, development, or growth you can think of—at any level of organization— that will not soon turn lethal if there is no countervailing tendency in the system. All health is, in this sense, dependent on oppositional complementarity. This is an ecological axiom which applies to all varieties of systems and has found expression in religion, in politics, in biology, in astronomy— to name a few.

It is also the idea expressed by the process of a dialectic, both in the lucid way Socrates practiced it and the opaque way Hegel explained it. Intellectual and cultural advance is made not through argument but through argument and counterargument. For the counterargument makes the deficiencies of the argument visible and makes improvement and synthesis possible. Without counterargument there is no way to govern error, excess, or distortion; there is nothing for an argument to measure itself against or limit itself by. The Greeks gave us still another word to work with here, for their word for "governor" or "steersman" is *kybernetes*, from which we derive the word cybernetics.

Cybernetics is merely a synonym for ecology. It is the science of control and equilibrium, the study of "feedback," which is not a Greek word but which nonetheless calls our attention to the means by which we maintain balance in a system. To Norbert Wiener, who invented the science of feedback, the clearest example of cybernetics-in-action—that is, the principle of oppositional complementarity—is a thermostat, a mechanism for triggering opposing forces. To a thermostat, it is a matter of indifference whether an environment be warm or cold. Assuming the thermostat has been set at a sane and healthful temperature, its job is to make what is too warm cooler and too cool warmer. A thermostat, in short, releases a counterargument. One might say it is in a dialectical relationship with its environment, and for this reason it provides an apt metaphor for the educational function I wish here to introduce and develop: *Education is best conceived of as a thermostatic activity.*

From this point of view, and stated far too grossly, education tries to conserve tradition when the rest of the environment is innovative. Or it is innovative when the rest of the society is tradition-bound. It is a matter of indifference whether the society be volatile or static. The function of education is always to offer the counterargument, the other side of the picture. The thermostatic view of education is, then, not ideology-centered. It is balance-centered. It is not so much a philosophy as it is a metaphilosophy—a philosophy about philosophies. Its aim at all times is to make visible the prevailing biases of a culture and then, by employing whatever philosophies of education are available, to oppose them. In the thermostatic view of education, you do not "hold" philosophies. You deploy them.

I imagine that this function of education will seem unsatisfactory to you if you are of a teleological turn of mind, if you believe that there is some special purpose that our culture is striving to achieve or that it ought to strive to achieve. In that case you will want education to further that end at all times, and to keep at it until the end is in view. You could hardly approve of any plan to oppose the fulfillment of such a purpose. But the thermostatic view speaks against such an outlook. It assumes that the business of a culture is to keep itself in working order, as steady and as balanced as possible. This is the ecological rather than the teleological outlook, for the ecologist never assumes that a forest, an ocean, a species, or indeed a society has purposes that must be achieved. The ecologist is not a utopian, not an ideologue, not a dogmatist, not a theologian. He is, rather, a physician, a navigator, a steersman. His politics is the politics of remediation. The only item on his agenda is to correct our imbalances.

The compelling need for such a view is argued by the fact that there are two well-known ways for a system to die. It may die from underactivity and stasis. Or it may die from strenuousness and instability. The aborigine culture I have referred to has survived as long as it has only because it remained isolated from any contact with a new idea or new artifact. One cannot deny that in its continuous and repeatable social patterns, it achieved a homeostatic relationship with its environment. But that environment extends only a few miles in its radius and is of such limited variety and opportunity that it is inevitable that the first contact with another culture will be close to lethal. Had the aborigines prepared themselves through an education that argued, even quietly, the virtue of innovation, their chances of surviving would now be much enhanced. As it is, the aborigines have overdosed, so to speak, on stability.

Our own culture is overdosing on change. One may call it "future shock," "culture shock," "technology shock," or whatever. The plain fact is that too much change, too fast, for too long has the effect of making social institutions useless and individuals perpetually unfit to live amid the conditions of their own culture. Since you have heard it all before, I will not bore you by cataloguing the technological changes which have come in Toffleresque profusion and have led to such Kafkaesque confusion. It is enough to say that we have reached the point where the problem of conservation, not growth, must now be solved. We know very well how to change but we have lost the arts of preservation. Without at least a reminiscence of continuity and tradition, without a place to stand from which to observe change, without a counterargument to the overwhelming thesis of change, we can easily be swept away—in fact, are being swept away.

To provide ourselves with such a perspective, we must rely on our education system. It is, after all, almost the only agency in our society which has no vested interest in change itself. For our schools, there is no money to be made from change, nor prestige to be gained from it. Progress is not the schools' most important product. Schools are, in fact, always given a measure of responsibility to serve as a society's memory bank, even in quiet times. In a society of great stability and firm tradition such a responsibility may be quite irrelevant since the entire culture is engaged in remembering, if not reliving, its past. The conserving function of school is, then, redundant and, according to the thermostatic view, even dangerous. However, in a culture of high volatility and casual regard for its past such a responsibility becomes the school's most essential service. *The school stands as the only mass medium capable of putting forward the case for what is not happening in the culture.* The last thing that teaching needs to be in our present situation is revolutionary, ground-breaking, and highly charged with new values. That is the voice in which our culture speaks. Who shall speak in a different voice?

In espousing the thermostatic conception of education, I do not claim for it or myself any originality. It is a venerable idea, at least twenty-three hundred years old, originating with Plato and extending into our own times wherein some of our best and some of our worst minds have embraced it. Among the best, for example, is David Riesman, who has preferred to name it "the countercyclical" theory of educa-tion and who has taken the trouble in a lifetime of work to identify some of the more powerful biases of our culture. From *The Lonely Crowd* to *Individualism Reconsidered* to *Constraint and Variety in American Education,* Riesman has either explicitly or by implication argued the case for educa-tional programs that would serve as ballast to the prevailing winds.

Where, for example, a culture is stressing autonomy and aggressive individuality, education should stress cooperation and social cohesion. Where a culture is stressing conformity, education should stress individuality. "All value," Riesman has said, "is contextual," by which he means that not even the noblest ideal or the clearest truth is unarguable. Bereft of serious opposition, our ideals and truths lose their vitality and, eventually, their meaning.[1] That so few have paid much attention to him is probably a tribute to the quiet, scholarly precision of his analyses. The clarity of his ideas far exceeds the loudness of their expression, and too many seem inclined to attend to loud, not clear, speakers. Which is why almost everyone has paid attention to the demands of those who align themselves with what is called the Back to the Basics Movement. This, too, is a warning against one-sided tendencies in our culture. But it is nothing more than that, for it has not been preceded by a careful analysis of what the tendencies are or followed by measured suggestions as to how they may be countered. Whereas "back to the basics" might be profitable as a question—an impetus to inquiry— it is, instead, commonly put forward as a conclusion or, worse, a slogan. And a threatening one at that. There is in every "back to the basics" proposal I have ever heard a badly concealed hostility toward both the young and their teachers. This is not, therefore, an authentic thermostatic or counter-cyclical view of education. It is rather a sociology of revenge in which one evens the score—for what affronts we can only guess—by piling pointless difficulty upon pointless difficulty.

As I write, the consequences of such reactions (they can hardly be called thinking) are to be seen almost everywhere: No automatic promotions. Tougher and more standardized tests. Strict behavioral measurements. A return to grammar. More expulsions from school. More severe and "objective" judgments of teachers.

I do not say categorically that all such measures are futile. If in a panic to cure an unspecified but worrisome disease, you pull antidotes at random from your medicine cabinet, it is not impossible that one or two may by chance be helpful. More likely you will merely obscure and compound the disease. It is much to be preferred that we diagnose with some precision what the problem is and select the exact remedies for it. What we are trying to help, it must be remembered, are our children, and not our own pathologies.

The danger of mindless opposition is what Lawrence Cremin undoubtedly had in mind when he argued against Riesman's "countercyclical" theory in *The Genius of American Education*.[2] In substance, Cremin complained that any thermostatic theory runs the risk of opposing everything indiscriminately. In this Cremin is correct, although Riesman had no such idea in mind. Nor do I. Education cannot offer a countervailing view of everything in a society; first, because no society would support such an effort; second, because not every tendency in society requires opposition from schools, either because it is already being opposed by some other institution or because it is not yet sufficiently troublesome to merit the respect of opposition. And third, and most important, because schools are simply not well suited to perform such a massive undertaking. Not only can they not provide what the home or church or economy or political system ought rightfully to provide (assuming we can agree on what this is), they cannot realistically oppose all the obvious excesses and mistakes of such institutions. For example, it has been argued by Christopher Lasch that the law, once regarded as embodying the moral consensus of the community, is now perceived as merely a technique for controlling behavior.[3] If he is right, or even half right, that law has been emptied of its moral content and replaced by an ethic of human relations, this is a very serious matter. But it is difficult to see how schools can effectively counter such a trend. Kenneth Keniston, to take another example, has revealed in his study of the American family that one out of every three children in America now grows up in a one-parent family. This fact obviously has serious psychological and social consequences. But I do not see how schools can deal with such a state of affairs. This is not to say that educators should not consider the question. They should, but their reflections ought to proceed with a sober regard for the limitations of education and certainly without high expectations. Every culture takes pleasure in its own methods of suicide, and the thermostatic view of education is on no account to be confused with the utopian view of education. Of all of this, there is much more to say, and I will try my hand at it later. What is being put forward here are three questions which comprise the heart of this book. The first is, What specific cultural biases, if left unchecked, will leave our youth with incompetent intellects and distorted personalities? The second is, To what extent is formal education competent to deal with such biases? The third is, How may education oppose, both emphatically and constructively, such biases as the school can hope to address?

The assumption implicit in each of these questions is that the major role of education in the years immediately ahead is to help conserve that which is both necessary to a humane survival and threatened by a furious and exhausting culture. That is why I have titled this book *Teaching as a Conserving Activity*. But it occurs to me now that, since I am talking about a program for subverting the prevailing biases of the culture, one may reasonably think of the book as titled *Teaching as a Subversive Activity*. I would not argue the point, except to say that a long time ago it seemed to me that only by looking ahead could we equip our children to face the present. It now seems to me that we might do it better by looking back. For a while.

The
Problems

2

The Information Environment

When I talk of education as a thermostat, I am of course using a metaphor. But the question arises nonetheless, What is it that the thermostat must act upon? What is it that needs to be warmed or cooled? to be adjusted and balanced? The answer comes as another metaphor: the information environment.

Every society is held together by certain modes and patterns of communication which control the kind of society it is. One may call them information systems, codes, message networks, or media of communication. Taken together they set and maintain the parameters of thought and learning within a culture. Just as the physical environment determines what the source of food and exertions of labor shall be, the information environment gives specific direction to the kinds of ideas, social attitudes, definitions of knowledge, and intellectual capacities that will emerge.

For example, there are people, like the aborigines, whose repertoire of communication possibilities consists almost entirely of talking to each other, face to face. The word is never isolated from the body that produces it. There is, therefore, always an immediate and specific context in which meaning is shared. Feedback is never an issue; communication always includes response. This situation gives both their interactions and their thought a high degree of subjectivity, spontaneity, and emotion. But it does not provide an occasion or stimulus for sustained speculation. Without disembodied words there is no disinterested thought. Everyone is, so to speak, an existentialist.

Introduce hieroglyphics or, if you can imagine it, a tape recorder to such people and you will alter their information environment, and with it, the sort of people they will be. When a medium of communication has the power to disembody words, to split them away from their original source, the psychological and social effects of language are forever changed. In such an environment, language becomes something more than a mode of communication. It becomes an object of contemplation. One may look at it, as in a mirror, and study how it is put together, with the result that the mind itself may become an object of contemplation. At which point philosophers (not to mention grammarians) must emerge to reflect on reflection and on what might be the connection between language and reality. Everyone may become a Platonist.

Or this may happen: Let us assume an aborigine has conceived of a way to chisel a message on stone. The message being more durable than its author, it will become more important than he, and will be read and reread over centuries. In such a situation, we should not be surprised if readers not only dispute the meaning of the message but ponder the meaning of time, and then of mortality itself. It is in fact not uncommon for people whose messages have endured, unchanging, for centuries to become obsessed with time, as were the ancient Egyptians and the Mayans.

And this may happen, too: A few will learn the symbols in which the message is encoded, and most will not. Thus, the few will be in possession of information to which the many have no access. The few will have, or seem to have (which is the same thing in this case), enormous and secret powers. Thus, priests will emerge to whom special privileges will be given and in whom there will reside special powers of explanation and authority.

And suppose it happens that someone, through accident or design, discovers that messages do not need to be chiseled in stone but can be scratched on a leaf or a reed. To be sure, not a very durable medium but one that can be carried far and wide and with considerable speed. Perhaps then the obsession with time will recede, to be replaced by a fascination with the mysteries of space. Thus, explorers and conquerors may emerge, and messages will tell of things happening in other places but maintain silence on what has happened in other times.

I shall not speak here of what may happen if you introduce television to a culture such as ours. That is the subject of the next chapter. What this chapter is about is the idea that the means by which people communicate comprise an environment just as real and influential as the terrain on which they live. And further: that when there occurs a radical shift in the structure of that environment this must be followed by changes in social organization, intellectual predispositions, and a sense of what is real and valuable. And further still: that it is the business of the educator to assess the biases of the information environment with a view toward making them visible and keeping them under control. A society that is unaware of what its information environment is leading to may become overwhelmed by philosophers, priests, conquerors, or even explorers. Or it may forget how to remember. Or may confine its imagination only to what it *can* remember. I mean to imply in every word of this book that it is the business of education, at all times, to monitor and adjust the information environment wherever possible so that its inherent biases and drift do not monopolize the intellect and character of our youth.

No one knew this better than Plato. All philosophy, Whitehead remarked, is only a footnote to Plato. Perhaps all education, as well. But if that is too much to say, Plato at least provides us with the first and one of the best illustrations of the thermostatic response to the information environment. He does it by banishing poets from his curriculum. He gives as his reason that poets, including Homer himself, do not always tell the truth about the gods, and further, that their influence is powerful. He completes the syllogism by concluding that a powerful influence that does not tell the truth ought not to be included in the formal education of the young. At this level of argument, Plato sounds like a modern-day fundamentalist arguing against the teaching of evolution in the schools. This is not the sort of idea that needs conserving right now, and if we stay at this level, Plato has very little to teach us.

But if one probes deeper, as has, for example, Eric Havelock, something else emerges. Plato, it turns out, was as much concerned with the effects of the form of epic poetry —indeed, with the form of any kind of information—as with its content, and in this respect his argument has the greatest possible importance to our own situation. Plato, like ourselves, was facing a critical shift in the structure of information within his culture. As an educationist of a thermostatic persuasion, he vigorously addressed the problems attending that shift—as I believe we must do—and it is worth taking the time to see what we may learn from him.

In his *Preface to Plato,* Havelock reminds us that although the Greek alphabet was perhaps four hundred years old at the time Plato wrote *The Republic,* Athens was still only semiliterate. Greek youth did not always learn to read, and those who did began their instruction in adolescence, not in their early years. There certainly did not exist a rich supply of texts to read, and such reading as was necessary was confined to public documents and inscriptions. The poets were writers, of course, but their poems were composed to be heard, not read, and the finished product was either recited or acted. The fact is that the culture which Plato was dealing with was one in which oral communication still dominated all the important transactions in life.

Moreover, their oral literature did not serve the same function for Athenian youth as literature came to serve later —for either the Greeks or us. In Plato's time, literature was the major means through which the traditions of the culture were transmitted. Its purpose, therefore, was more didactic than diversionary. (The Greek word from which we derive *epic* meant, simply, *discourse.*) There being no textbooks to read, no reference books to consult, no monographs to peruse, the Athenian student had to memorize vast and complex quantities of Homeric poetry, the result of which provided him with a complete history of the symbols and values of his culture. He was, so to speak, a living, mobile library.

But how could such feats of memory be achieved? Our own youth can hardly be counted on to memorize "Paul Revere's Ride." If you ask them, also, to memorize *Hiawatha,* you have pushed them over the precipice. The answer, and the difference, lies in the form of information and the context in which it is experienced. In a phrase, the information environment. Today, all written literature, even poetry, is intended to be read—seen with the eye—and largely experienced in isolation from others. This was not the case in Plato's time. Poetry, as I have mentioned, was to be heard and was almost always experienced through public performances. Frequently, it was done to the accompaniment of a harp, an audio (but not visual) aid which is used to this very day to augment TV or radio commercial messages. We do not use a harp, of course, but Plato would understand very well why commercial messages are sung or at least recited with a musical background. Rhythm assists remembering, and he would be quick to point out that it also "cripples the intellect." But that is slightly ahead of the story.

In Plato's time the memorizing power of youth was enhanced not only through music but in many ways, including constant repetition in every available context—at banquets, at family rituals, in the market place, and at the theater. And, of course, the youth themselves were performers, acting their epics as they heard them acted whenever possible. Performance and poetry were inseparable. This meant that the young were involved emotionally and subjectively with the content of their discourses to a degree we would find difficult to grasp. Today, we wish our young to "appreciate" literature and to exercise their own judgment in evaluating its merit. Athenian youth were concerned to reproduce their literature, not reflect upon it. They did not so much evaluate characters and their situations as they identified with them and relived their experience. A sense of critical detachment was not only unnecessary, it was undesirable. As Havelock says: "You threw yourself into the situation of Achilles, you identified with his grief or his anger. You yourself became Achilles. . . . Thirty years later you could automatically quote what Achilles had said or what the poet had said about him. Such enormous powers of poetic memorization could be purchased only at the cost of total loss of objectivity."

A total loss of objectivity! This was the price to be paid for the perpetuation of the history of the society. It is a price an oral culture always must pay. And it was this state of affairs, this learning style, this use of the intellect, to which Plato objected and which led him to banish the poets. As Walter Ong remarks: "Plato was telling his compatriots that it was foolish to imagine that the intellectual needs of life in Greek society could still be met by memorizing Homer."[1]

Plato meant to provide Greek youth with an alternative curriculum, one which emphasized abstract thought as against concrete imagery, and critical detachment as against subjective involvement. He meant to prepare Greek youth for the psychological and intellectual biases of the written word and to wean them from their orientation to the spoken word.

Plato grasped that writing, by providing us with a trans-personal memory, not only made ritualized memorizing pointless but opened the way to new uses of the intellect. The inscription over his Academy, "Let none enter who knows not geometry," was a rebuke to the biases of epic poetry and an invitation to exploit the abstract, disembodied, highly visual bias of the written symbol. For, as Plato knew, the written word directs our attention to symbols rather than things. Because the phonetic symbol always refers to things that are not present and most often to things we do not know about, it permits us to go (to quote Harold Innis) "beyond the world of concrete experience into the world of conceptual relations." Moreover, we travel to and in that world through the eye, by seeing the symbols of our symbols. Writing freezes, as with a still camera, the fluid, nonrepeatable mo-ments of speech, and fixes our thought in space as well as in time. Through the alphabet, we can see our mind at work, reflect on its processes, and put it in order. Almost all of our methods of classifying, comparing, and contrasting presup-pose a visual, stabilized abstraction of speech. The word "idea" itself means visual image, the look of things. Homeric Greek does not contain the word "ideos" from which it is derived. Idea is a product of literacy. One may even wish to go as far as Marshall McLuhan and say that *mind* itself is a consequence of literacy.

The spoken word—rhythmic, aural, subjective, resonant, always in the present—versus the written word—cold, vi-sual, abstract, objective, timeless. This was the conflict, the invisible issue which generated an education crisis. What was at stake here was not the virtue of Greek youth but their intellect, for Plato knew that the dominant form of information in a culture shapes the intellectual orientation of its citizens. As a matter of fact, so did his teacher, Socrates. In the *Phaedrus,* Socrates speaks sharply against the intrusions of the written word. He explains that writing will reduce the power of our memories. Which it did. That it will make dialectic impossible since it forces us to follow an argument rather than to participate in it. Which it does. And finally, that writing will undermine our concepts of privacy and social propriety since it is a "mass medium" of sorts. To quote him: "Once a word is written, it goes rolling all about, comes indifferently among those who understand it and those whom it no wise concerns, and is unaware to whom it should address itself and to whom it should not do so."[2]

Both Socrates and Plato, then, were fully aware of the shaping power of a new means of communication. Those who think that "the medium is the message" is a modern conception should note that twenty-three hundred years ago both Plato and Socrates in speaking of writing addressed themselves to what the written word, irrespective of its content, is capable of doing to a culture. But, of course, teacher and student were on opposite ends of the education argument. Socrates was the oral man, the discourse man, the defender of the powers and biases of the human dialectic. He wrote no books himself, and were it not for Xenophon and Plato, who did, we would know almost nothing of him. Plato was the writing man, the scientific man, the promoter of the powers and biases of the written word. He not only wrote about Socrates but prepared the texts he wished Greek youth to study, and even suggested that reading instruction should begin at four years of age. Plato prevailed, of course. By the end of the Peloponnesian War, Athens had passed through its stage of semiliteracy, and entered a period of visual thinking and learning on which all of its education became based and on which all Western education remained based for over two thousand years.[3]

What we may learn from all of this has, as I have said, the greatest possible relevance to our own situation. We may see, first of all, the sense in which Plato was putting forward a thermostatic view of education. His culture being in the thrall of the oral tradition, he stressed the virtues of the written word. That he was in this circumstance a revolutionary, not a conservative, is irrelevant. To everything there is a season, and a time to every education under heaven. Had Plato been born a hundred years later perhaps he would have tried to foster the values of epic poetry and its memorization. Perhaps he would have filled his school with harps and the words of the poets, and would have inscribed over his Academy, "Let none enter who knows not Homer." There is, in fact, some reason to believe in the plausibility of that idea. In his Seventh Letter, Plato remarks that "no man of intelligence will venture to express his philosophical views in language, especially not in language that is unchangeable, which is true of that which is set down in written characters." And, of course, we must remember that it is Plato who wrote the arguments against writing that we attribute to Socrates.

Plato, in other words, saw both sides of the picture. He knew the value of both speech and writing, but in the context of that time and place, he decided in favor of the written word. And he so decided because it was the spoken word that controlled the minds of the young. The written word was to release them from its grip. Though Plato did not say it, he must have believed that at that juncture the function of education was to free the young from the tyranny of the past. Sometimes the function of education is to free the young from the tyranny of the present. It depends on what is the character of the information environment. That is the essence of the thermostatic view of education.

But we are not finished with Plato. He teaches us still other things. He knew, for example, what so many contemporary educators are ignorant of—that a curriculum is not something only found in school. One's culture is a curriculum, or rather, a conglomerate of curriculums. For what is a curriculum but a design for controlling and shaping the minds of the young? It is not in opposition to the existing Athenian *school* curriculum that Plato offered his alternative. It is to the Athenian culture itself. The banquets, the marketplace, the theater—these are the curriculums Plato had his eye upon. A school curriculum that is only an alternative to another school curriculum amounts to very little. It is an invention of teachers who are bored with what *they* are doing. What is necessary is an alternative to what the culture is doing.

And how does one know what a culture is doing? This, too, Plato teaches us. At least he shows us where to look, directing our attention to the structure of information within society. We may infer that Plato knew that the imagery, character, and ideology of every society are not only shaped by but created by its dominant means of forming, retaining, and distributing information. But perhaps Plato did not know, as many have learned since, how complex the structure of information is, for it is comprised of several properties, all of which are interrelated.

Information, first and foremost, has form; it is generated by a particular coding system and through the use of certain materials which make our symbols tangible and give them life. Speech itself is surely the most important of all information forms, and it hardly needs to be said that without speech, very little information can be created. Through speech our species became information creators, gatherers, and sharers of the highest order. It is, however, worth noting that languages themselves differ vastly in their form and as a consequence produce different kinds and categories of information about the world. The language of the Hopi Indians is structured so differently from our own that we must expect that Hopis will not see the world quite the way we do. Their language, for example, does not conceive of time by the same metaphors as does our own, and the aspects of reality their language directs them to name and classify are by no means the same as in our own coding system. Language, as many anthropologists have shown, is not merely a means of communicating. It is also an organ of perception. It creates the world as much as reflects it by calling our attention to some parts of it and by turning us away from other parts. This much we have known or at least suspected for centuries.

But beyond this, we have not sufficiently understood the extent to which our other coding systems are also windows to the world, filled with optical illusions and peculiar refractions. It makes a difference in our perceptions of the world and our attentions to it whether we are chiseling ideographs on stone tablets or scratching phonetically alphabetized words on papyrus. In fact it even makes a difference if the alphabet we are using has no vowels (as in the case of the Semitic alphabet) or if it does (as in the case of the Greek).

It makes a difference because information is not reality. It is an abstraction of it. How high the abstraction or how low, how durable or transient, how precise or gross, how systematic or undifferentiated, how easily repeatable or unique— these will all be settled by the code and its associated material. The printing press, the computer, and television are not therefore simply machines which convey information. They are metaphors through which we conceptualize reality in one way or another. They will classify the world for us, sequence it, frame it, enlarge it, reduce it, argue a case for what it is like. Through these media-metaphors, we do not see the world as it is. We see it as our coding systems are. Such is the power of the form of information.

But information also has quantity or magnitude. How much information we may get depends of course on the forms in which it is available. "Of the making of many books," it is written in Ecclesiastes, "there is no end." Imagine what this overburdened reader might have thought about a society in which thousands of books are published every year, and thousands of copies of each one. Think for a moment of how much we depend on a constant supply of information in order to complete one day in our lives without disaster. Think also of all the institutions that exist solely for the purpose of processing and distributing information. From this point of view, we are surely permitted to say that our social institutions do not create information. It is information that creates our social institutions. Moreover, the problems of a society with an insufficient amount of information are entirely different from those of a society with too much information. Both societies, however, may collapse, one from emaciation, the other from satiation.

Information also has speed or velocity. It makes a difference in what we make of the world if information moves slowly, as in oral cultures, or at the speed of light, as in electronic cultures. It makes a difference, too, in which directions the information moves, who has access to it, and in what sorts of circumstances. In short, not only do our media-metaphors direct our attention to selected aspects of reality but they do it fast or slow, in large or small amounts, and by delegating certain roles for us to play in the process.

In reading this book, for example, you have most likely isolated yourself from others, seated yourself, tried to shut down your ears, and have agreed to follow my arguments, such as they are, line by line, page by page. The left hemisphere of your brain is exceedingly active and is engaged in reflection and analysis. The muscles of your eyes will soon enough begin to tire, which will limit the duration of your involvement. At that point, should you wish to express an important disagreement with what I have written, you will not have access to the one person most in need, however reluctantly, of your opinion. Me. If you knew my telephone number, you could get your opinion to me with great speed and with the unique sense of conviction and urgency that only the human voice can convey. At the same time, in speaking with me on the phone, you will have entered, with me, into a strange world of acoustic space in which disembodied voices exchange information intimately and in specially developed personas. If you cannot reach me by telephone, you may write a letter, but it will be slow in arriving, and I am not compelled to answer or I can pretend not to understand. In any case, we will be separated by an impressive psychological distance which I should not fail to exploit.

Think of it all for a moment: How strange are the forms in which information is created and reality abstracted—in sounds, scribbles, dots, pictures, electronic impulses. And what materials they require—paper of variable textures, ink, screens, lights, punches, discs. And how much of it we may get and in what sequences. And think especially of what is required of our brains, senses, and bodies to get it. We must sit in dark palaces or well-lit living rooms. Light may come from behind a screen or in front of it. Pictures intersect sentences. We must go back in time or ahead of it. Or time may be suspended, contracted, or expanded. And think of how slowly some forms of information move and how rapidly do others. And think of where these forms come from and to whom they are addressed. Surely it is not too much to say that the configuration of all these properties of information has the deepest physiological, psychological, and social consequences. Nor is it too much to say—in fact, it is saying the same thing—that the configuration of these properties at any given time and place comprises an invisible environment around which we form our ideas about time and space, learning, knowledge, and social relations.

For example, a society in which law is codified in written words thinks differently about property, contracts, and obligations from a society in which law exists only in memory.

"A single copy of the Twelve Tables has greater weight and authority than all the philosophies of the world," Cicero wrote. This is an idea that was incomprehensible to the Anglo-Saxons when brought to them by the Romans, as indeed it is incomprehensible to our contemporary aborigines. Perhaps it is no longer even comprehensible to us. Living, as we do, in an electronic world of pictures and sounds, can the written word have the same power with which we once invested it? In saying this, I do not mean to imply that written law is more civilized than oral law. Only that they represent different conceptions of social constraint and obligation, separated from each other by the metaphysics of two modes of communication.

A society in which sacred knowledge is codified in complex pictographs to which few have access develops different religious sentiments and institutions from those of a society whose sacred knowledge is codified in an alphabet to which many have access. And, of course, a society in which television is used does not have sacred knowledge at all. For sacred knowledge implies monopolistic knowledge, esoteric knowledge, mystical knowledge, hierarchical knowledge. Television, by its nature, implacably opposes such a conception. In an information environment with television at the center, there can be no kabalas and few state secrets. Have we not become accustomed to the unholy spectacle of parish priests instructing the Pope in the ways of both God and man? And is it not so that two of our recent presidents suffered the unexpected indignity of having to flee their office because they could not control the privacy and movement of information? The electric plug is more than a hole in the wall. It is the entrance through which an entire population penetrates secret chambers.

Moreover, it is obvious that in a culture where information is shared in face-to-face contexts, is moved slowly, and is sluggishly disseminated, there will not be a knowledge explosion. But it is equally obvious that where information is codified in electronic impulses and moved at the speed of light, there must be a knowledge explosion. Is it any wonder that Socrates believed that all useful knowledge must be drawn from *inside* us?—for that is where speech itself comes from. And that we believe that all useful knowledge must come from *outside* us?—for our media are not part of us but external to us. "The unexamined life is not worth living," Socrates said. "The unexamined world is not worth living in," we reply. The very definition of knowledge in any era is a function of the form, magnitude, speed, direction, and accessibility of information.

Similarly, political ideas are a function of information patterns. Thomas Jefferson wondered why the Athenians to whom we are indebted for the creation of democracy did not also conceive of the idea of representative government. That the will of an individual could be expressed indirectly and abstractly through an elected official made no sense in Athens. It seemed perfectly obvious in Monticello. Such a difference in outlook can be accounted for by our remembering that the oral dialectic, by its nature, is concerned with individual action and feeling. It always involves personal contact and immediate response. On the other hand, the written word, as Innis remarks of the newspaper, addresses the world, not the individual. A reading person will accept abstract, indirect government. A dialectic person will not even imagine it.

I realize I am on the verge of committing the fallacy of reductionism, for I feel the strongest impulse to say that the structure of information can account for anything that occurs in a culture. But this would be nonsense. Instead, I will settle for this view of the matter: The dominant patterns of information within a culture—the codes, the materials, the styles of interaction they require—form a substantial part of the "genes" of a culture. Like genes, information patterns produce in mysterious ways the general features of a culture, and in something approximating a predictable pattern. Like genes, information patterns are powerful but not entirely resistant to modification (or what's education for?). And like genes, information patterns do their work invisibly. We scarcely know they are there until a mutation occurs. It is only when a culture has undergone a restructuring of its information patterns that we can see on what its intellectual and social biases previously rested.

Isaac Taylor, for example, in his great work, *The History of the Alphabet,* has shown how the change in the form of writing—from ideograph to alphabet—made information available to people to whom it had previously been denied. Thus, not only did both religion and science fall out of the exclusive control of the priestly class but the gap between rulers and ruled diminished. Both Lewis Mumford and Jacques Ellul have shown how the invention of the mechanical clock, by totally reconstructing our image of time and space, laid the foundation of all modern forms of social organization. A sun dial does not give you the same information as does a mechanical clock. The difference in their level of abstraction, their precision, and the context in which the information becomes accessible gave us a new metaphor for the universe. The precise segmenting of time in a transportable form makes possible, and urgent, the question, "Exactly what time is it?" For time-keeping, as Mumford tells us, "passed into time-serving and time-accounting and time-rationing. Eternity ceased gradually to serve as the measure and focus of human actions." By separating time from human events, the clock helped us to conceive of an independent world of measurable sequences; that is, the world as modern science conceives of it.

We are people of the clock, as we have been people of the printed page. But to appreciate what we were like before the printed page, one must read a book such as *The Bias of*

Communication by Harold Innis, in which he shows how print altered almost every conceivable facet of social, political, and economic life. He argues, for example, that the printing press undermined the information monopoly of the Catholic Church, not only by making the Word of God accessible to large numbers of people but by moving it with unprecedented speed throughout Germany, and then the rest of Europe. He has also shown how print, by isolating the reader and his responses, created a psychological context which fostered the growth of modern forms of capitalism. And Phillipe Ariès in his *Centuries of Childhood* has suggested, by implication, an additional and astonishing effect of the printing press: The rapid buildup and movement of secular information made possible by print not only created the modern concept of education but, in so doing, created the modern concept of childhood itself.

All of these revolutionary changes in the structure of society were precipitated, at least to a significant extent, by mutations in the structure of information. Change the form of information, or its quantity, or speed, or direction, or accessibility, and some monopoly will be broken, some ideology threatened, some pattern of authority will find itself without a foundation. We might say that the most potent revolutionaries are those people who invent new media of communication, although typically they are not aware of what they are doing. When Gutenberg announced that he could manufacture books, as he put it, "without the help of reed, stylus, or pen but by wondrous agreement, proportion, and harmony of punches and types," he could scarcely imagine that he had just become the most important political and social troublemaker of the Second Millennium. Unless that dubious title be given to Professor Samuel Morse who, in sparking the electronic revolution under whose conditions we must now live, at least had the good grace to wonder, What hath God wrought? Well, God hath wrought plenty, and in the next chapter I want to begin identifying the specific biases of the Morsian Revolution; that is, the configuration of our present information patterns. Here, I wish to conclude by making two observations, both of which I have already stated but which bear repeating. The first is that it is always necessary to provide a balance to the information biases of a culture. Such biases, if left unchecked, are tyrannies, closing off our awareness of different metaphors of the world and of different opportunities for understanding and expression. Societies strangle themselves by unrelieved information bigotry. As Dean Inge once remarked, civilization is a disease almost invariably fatal unless the cause is checked in time. The cause is as much the biases of information as anything else.

Second, it is the main business of education to know what these biases are and to know what to balance them with. I shall go so far as to say that the subject of education consists of little else than the analysis of communication forms, the interpretation of their psychological and social effects, and the development of school environments which supply a balance to such effects. When I talk about education, I am talking about the information life of our children. When I talk about a thermostatic view of education, I am talking about the sane management of their information life. If there is anything else to the matter, I do not know what it is.

3

The First
Curriculum

The educational problem now comes into focus. We must determine as best we can what sort of people our modern forms of information are producing. Then we must come up with some careful plans to counterbalance those effects that are clearly one-sided and which without opposition and mitigation are likely to be disabling to our youth. In the manner of Plato, we may have to banish some forms of communication from the schools altogether.

In this chapter, we begin our search for such effects by concentrating on what is surely the single most powerful new element in our information environment, television. Everybody seems to know (except its executives) that television is exerting a profound influence on our youth, although we are not always clear as to what it is. I propose, in this and the chapter that follows, to suggest the nature of that influence, and to begin doing so by comparing television with another and older medium of communication, school. As it is mostly conducted even in the present age, school is one of our few remaining information systems firmly organized around preelectronic patterns of communication. School is old times and old biases. For that reason, it is more valuable to us than most people realize, but, in any case, provides a clear contrast to the newer system of perception and thought that television represents. By putting television and school side by side, we can see where we are going and what we are leaving, which is exactly what we need to know.

I will here anticipate a conclusion to be drawn later by saying that the traditional school (as I shall depict it) has much less wrong with it than I once believed; that is, it has much less wrong with it *in the age of television and other electronic media.* According to the thermostatic view, what is right or wrong with school is to be judged contextually by the effects of the surrounding media. If a traditional school exerts influences that make visible and modify the biases of new media, then it is obviously an institution to be aggressively preserved. This does not mean that such an institution cannot be improved, although not necessarily by making it more modern. In fact, as I shall also indicate later, one of the ways to improve school is by preventing it from becoming "modern." And this does not mean—I feel compelled to say again—going "back to the basics." Without their quite realizing it, advocates of the "basics" are, in some destructive ways, much more modern than they suppose, and, as I shall argue when discussing the Technical Thesis, are technocrats of the deepest commitment.

I might add here, as well, that in the competition between the biases of school and the biases of television, I have no doubt that the biases of the latter will prevail. This can safely be predicted not only because television is newer and more powerful by itself but because its effects are continuously reinforced by other media of communication, including records, tapes, radio, photography, and film. Thus, it is well to remember that in designing a thermostatic education, what one is trying to control is not which set of biases will win the competition but what the score will be. The narrower the margin, the better. If the theses of our past are entirely overwhelmed by the theses of the present, there is no possibility of a creative argument between the two, and therefore no way to control excess and misdirection in our future.

The first point, then, to be made about television and school is the Platonic observation that each of them is a curriculum. A curriculum, as commonly defined, is a course of study whose purpose is to train or cultivate both mind and character. Schools are generally acknowledged to *have* curriculums although typically it is not acknowledged that they *are* curriculums. But, of course, they are. Everything about a school has an effect—intentional or not—on the shaping of the young, and a "course of study" surely includes all of the conditions under which learning takes place. Sometimes these "conditions" are referred to as the "hidden curriculum," although from whom it is supposed to be hidden is not clear. The total school environment is the most visible thing about school and is certainly what is most remembered about school by everybody in later years. Television is not usually acknowledged either to have a curriculum or to be one, which is probably why parents do not pay as much attention to the television education of their children as they do to their school education. Many parents, as well as educators, seem to believe that television is an "entertainment medium," by which they mean to imply that little of enduring value is either taught by or learned from it.

But all of this can be seen in a clarifying light if we simply define a curriculum as a specially constructed information system whose purpose, *in its totality,* is to influence, teach, train, or cultivate the mind and character of our youth. By this definition, television and school not only have curriculums but are curriculums; that is, they are total learning systems. Each has a special way of organizing time and space; their messages are encoded in special forms and moved at different rates of speed; each has its special way of defining knowledge, its special assumptions about the learning process, and its own special requirements concerning how one must attend to what is happening. Moreover, each has a characteristic subject matter, ambience, and style, all of which reflect the unique context within which one experiences what is going on. And, of course, though their effects are strikingly different, each has as its purpose the control of our young. Viewed in this way, television is not only a curriculum but *constitutes the major educational enterprise now being undertaken in the United States.* That is why I call it the First Curriculum. School is the second.

Let us then get down to cases. The first thing a curriculum has to do is to engage the attention of its students for a certain period of time. Thus there are two questions to be addressed: how much time? and, how to get their attention? If we assume a child will go to school for thirteen years— say, starting in kindergarten and ending with high school— a typical American child will be in the presence of a school curriculum 2,340 days, which comes to about 11,500 hours. There are only two activities which occupy more of a youngster's time during those years. One of them is sleeping (which, by the way, is probably the real "hidden curriculum"). The other is attending to television. Studies of TV viewing are far from definitive but a fair estimate is that from age five to eighteen, an American child watches TV approximately 15,000 hours. That is thirty percent more time than he or she is engaged at school, a very significant difference considering the magnitudes involved. If we add to the 15,000 hours of TV viewing the time occupied by radio and record listening, as well as moviegoing, we come up with a figure very close to 20,000 hours of exposure to an electric medium curriculum, almost double the amount of time spent in school.

And so the television curriculum is first in the time given to it by students, and, as we shall see, it is also first in their hearts. Why this is so is related to the manner in which the two curriculums command attention. Both the school and the television curriculums use compulsion—the school directly through legal means, television indirectly through psychological means. If we ask what the roots of these different types of compulsions are, we arrive at some interesting answers. For instance, the school curriculum includes a content or subject matter selected, in principle, for its significant cultural or intellectual value. But its content may or may not be of interest to the student—in fact, traditionally is not—thus requiring legal force to compel attendance to it. Moreover, there is also a social and occupational basis to the compulsions of school. One must attend in order to get some place in life, especially if that place is college or a professional school. School is one step in a hierarchical structure which leads to heavenly and lucrative occupations. Or so it is generally believed. If compulsory education laws were repealed in every state, it would be fascinating to see who would continue to go to school and who would not, and what accommodations, if any, business and the professions would make.

In any case, the television curriculum is based on an entirely different principle of compulsion. Whereas the school curriculum compels attention through law and even occupational necessity, the TV curriculum requires no such external controls. *Television is an attention-centered curriculum.* In a certain sense, it has no goal other than keeping the attention of its students. Unlike the school, which selects its subject matter first and then tries to devise methods to attract interest in it, television first selects ways to attract interest, allowing content to be shaped accordingly. This is not to say that the content of the school curriculum is always significant or that the content of television is always trivial; only that, in the first instance, attention is subservient to content, and, in the second, content is wholly subservient to attention. In the school curriculum, if the student repeatedly does not pay attention, the teacher may remove him from class. In the TV curriculum, if the student repeatedly does not pay attention, the teacher is removed from class.

This is an exceedingly important bias because it means that the television curriculum does not have to concern itself with penalties. Most children, at least beyond a certain age, attend school largely to avoid the penalties for not doing so, whether the source be their parents, the law, or the future. School is, to a considerable extent, a penalty-laden curriculum, as is life itself, I've noticed. Not television. There is no penalty for not attending to one's TV lessons and none is needed. This fact surrounds the experience of television attendance with a benign psychological ambience that the school can never achieve.

One must also note that the TV curriculum has an additional advantage in gaining attention through what may be called the compulsions of proximity and continuousness; its lessons are easily accessible and for all practical purposes, endless. This is a point to which I want to return later in a different context. Here, it is necessary to turn our attention to the form in which information in each curriculum is codified. In order to do this properly, I must take you on a small side trip into the realm of symbolic or (as they are sometimes called) semiotic forms.

There are almost as many ways to categorize different types of signs and symbols as there are scholars who have done it. The complexities of the matter are such that there is no taxonomy of which I am aware that is not filled with ambiguity and even contradiction. But there is general agreement that there are at least two quite different types of symbols in which information is codified: analogic form and digital form. The differences between them must be grasped in order to understand the biases of both the television and the school curriculums.

Analogic forms of information are systems of codification

which have a real and intrinsic relationship to what they signify. A photograph is a good example. A picture of a man calls to mind the reality of that man because the picture itself is analogous in form to the man himself. The picture may be bigger or smaller than the man actually is, or even of a different color, but there is enough similarity between the structure of the man and the structure of the image so that one understands what is being represented. A map would be another good example of analogic symbolism. If, in reality, one road is twice as long as another, then a map will also depict it as twice as long. A good map, no matter what its scale, tries to be a structural analog to the territory it depicts. Analogic forms, in other words, have direct correspondences to the structure of nature itself. Such representations mimic, replicate, and specify, through their form, recognizable aspects of reality. On the other hand, digital forms of information are entirely abstract, and have no natural correspondences to nature. The word *man*, whether spoken or written, has no intrinsic relationship to that which it stands for. Here, the connection between symbolic form and the thing it represents is arbitrary. You cannot know what *man* refers to by your knowledge of nature alone. You must know the semantic code. And not only that. You must also know the structure by which words are connected to other words, for *a man kills a bear* does not mean the same thing as *a bear kills a man*. But in order for us to have a grammatical structure at all, we must rely on both the stability and portability of the meanings of our words. It is in the nature of digital symbolism to give us this assurance. All systems of digital symbols consist of small meaning units that can be displayed in different contexts and moved about in different positions. Their grammatical function may change in the process but there is an essential constancy to their lexical meaning. In digital systems, meanings are context-free (at least relatively so), which is why dictionaries are possible. In mathematics, which is also digital, we find exactly the same situation. The number 6, for example, will retain its meaning whether it is being used as a divisor or multiplier, or anything else. But this is not the case in analogic systems. Pictures, maps, and photographs are not reducible to vocabularies. The meaning of a line or contrasting areas of light is entirely dependent on the total context in which it appears and therefore a captive of that which is, in reality, being depicted. Analogic symbols have no meaning-units comparable in their constancy and portability to what we possess in digital systems. Thus, the meanings of digital forms have their origin in complex human conventions and binding human agreements. The meanings of analogic forms have their origin in our perceptions of the structure of nature and our capacity to copy its form.

All language, of course, is a digital form of information. In addition to its being arbitrary, abstract, and segmented, language has several other characteristics that distinguish it from analogues, two of which are especially important. The first is that words do not in fact call to mind specific referents. A word does not refer to a specific thing so much as it refers to a category of things; which is to say, words are concepts. When I say or write the word *man,* you do not know which man. What is brought to your mind is a concept of a man, a composite of possibilities. To be sure, I could use more words to give you a more specific idea of who or what I have in mind. But it is not possible, through language, to achieve a level of specificity which would make it unnecessary for you to have an *idea* about the words. Descriptive words such as the adjectives in "a tall, dark, handsome man" merely limit the concept of "man" by introducing additional concepts. As long as words are being used, we are always at a considerable remove from reality, for words are not representations of reality. They are representations of ideas about reality.

That is why (and this is the second point) all language is paraphrasable. By using different words, one can always approximate what someone else has said. If this were not so, there could be no such thing as translation. Translation can occur because an idea, unlike a picture, can be represented in various ways. Words have synonyms. Pictures do not. Analogic forms, such as pictures, are not ideas; nor are they paraphrasable. A picture must be experienced to be experienced. This is what people mean when they say, "You have to see it," or "You should have been there." They mean that the symbolic event must be directly apprehended in the form in which it exists. There is no translation of it. There is no idea of it. If you attempt to use a different form to convey the meaning, you will change the meaning. For example, you cannot use a picture of one man to represent a picture of another man. (Unless, of course, you tell someone, in language, that this is what you mean. And even then the "translation" will probably not work.) Each image is distinct and unique, and calls to mind only what is imaged. This is so precisely because of its concreteness and specificity. In fact, that is why there can be no picture of the concepts of *man* or *work* or *school.* There can only be images of specific men or specific kinds of work or schools. Moreover, the words "This is a picture of a lady with a faint smile" are not, *in any sense,* the equivalent of a painting of such a lady. Ten thousand words or a million will not translate into the picture. Words are of a different order of abstraction, requiring an entirely different mode of intellectual activity.

The image—concrete, unique, nonparaphrasable—versus the word—abstract, conceptual, translatable. This is one of several conflicts between TV and school, and perhaps the most important. For obvious reasons that have to do with the structure of television, its curriculum is essentially imagistic, that is, picture-centered. Its teaching style is therefore almost wholly narrative. To put it simply, the content of the

TV curriculum consists of picture stories. The school curriculum, on the other hand, tends to be word or concept-centered, and its teaching style, exposition. The school curriculum—at least in its content—consists of abstract propositions: linguistic statements of which we may say they are true or false, verifiable or not, logical or confused.

This is another way of saying that the TV curriculum does its work in analogic symbols which appeal directly to emotional and largely unreflective response, while the school curriculum, relying heavily on digital symbolism, requires sophisticated cognitive processing. It is not true, as so many have insisted, that watching TV is a passive experience. Anyone who has observed children watching television will know how foolish that statement is. In watching TV, children have their emotions fully engaged. It is their capacity for abstraction that is quiescent. In school the situation is apt to be reversed. For there, you are required, in principle, to understand and consider what is *said.* That means you are expected to be able to paraphrase, translate, and reformulate what is said, which is why tests are so easy to give in school. In experiencing TV, you are required to *feel* what is *seen,* which is why there can be no paraphrase and no meaningful test.

This difference between symbols that demand conceptualization and reflection and symbols that evoke feeling has many implications, one of the most important being that the content of the TV curriculum is irrefutable. You can dislike it but you cannot disagree with it. There is no way to refute Donny and Marie, or an Ajax commercial. The semiotic form of the TV curriculum is not in propositional form, does not deal in the sort of information that the symbols of the school curriculum do. Images and sentences are neither processed by the brain nor evaluated by the intelligence in the same way. They do different things and require different responses.

In this connection we must not be misled by the metaphorical uses of the word *statement* when it is used to apply to images. For example: Picasso has made a strong antiwar statement in "Guernica." "Statement" here means to evoke a feeling about war. It does not mean to make an assertion about it. "Guernica" is not a proposition. It is certainly not translatable or refutable. On the other hand, the series of literal statements that Picasso was born in Ketchum, Idaho, majored in dental mechanics at New York University, and married Rita Hayworth is both paraphrasable and (certainly) refutable. Similarly, the picture stories on television, including those of commercials, do not make "statements," except in the sense of evoking feelings. That is why, incidentally, the truth-in-advertising laws are mostly pointless. There is no way to show that the feelings evoked by the imagery of a McDonald's commercial are false, or indeed, true. Such words as *true* and *false* come out of a different universe of symbolism altogether. Propositions are true or false. Pictures are not.

In saying all of this, I am not ridiculing television but merely describing an important bias of the form of the medium. Television is not to be faulted because it consists of pictures. To do so would be like faulting an English sentence for having a subject and predicate. Nor can the television curriculum be faulted for its moralistic and value-laden bias. That is its nature. Narratives of any kind—in this case, picture stories—are inevitably aphoristic and metaphorical. Exposition, on the other hand, works through definition, assertion, explication, and analysis—an ensemble which by contrast with the form of narration is relatively value-neutral.

Let me put it this way: Consider the case of two professors. The first, Professor Neil Postman, talks about the thermostatic conception of education in his classes. He defines what it is and how it works. Through the medium of English sentences, he tries to use history, logic, and research to formulate, explain, and justify his ideas. His ideas are, of course, refutable by counterargument, which is the nature of exposition. One may say that there is value and even moral purpose in his goals. But he does not, and cannot, attach a moral implication to every word and fact and proposition. To do that would be to talk like Jesus; that is, to use language as parable.

On the other hand there is Professor Gabe Kaplan of *Welcome Back, Kotter.* Professor Kaplan is a teacher, too. But he does not work with facts, propositions, generalizations, or anything that is refutable. Like Jesus, he works almost wholly in parables. Of course, unlike Jesus', his parables are constructed not in language, which always contains a conceptual base, but in pictures. For though human speech is heard on television, it is the picture that always contains the most important meanings. Above all, people *watch* television. And so Kotter's parables are invariably encoded in dynamic, continuously shifting imagery. And like all parables, they are particularizations of a way of life, or a style of human relations, or a method of solving problems. *Charlie's Angels* and *M*A*S*H* are similarly parabolistic, and so is a commercial for United Airlines. That you may not like the drift of these parables is a question that we can turn to later. Here, it is well to remember that the Pharisees felt the same way about Jesus' parables but in the long run were powerless against them.

What it comes down to is this: Because the school curriculum's primary form of information is language, its style of teaching is expository. And because its style of teaching is expository, it concerns itself with facts and arguments. And because of that, it cannot help (even when its teaching is done badly) promoting concepts of knowledge and ways of knowing that stress the importance of detachment, objectivity, analysis, and criticism. In a sentence, the school curriculum is both rationalistic and secular in its outlook.

Television is both aesthetic and (at least) quasi-religious. Because its primary form of information is the image, its style of teaching is narration. And because of that, it is concerned with showing concrete people and situations toward which one responds by either accepting or rejecting them on emotional grounds. Television teaches you to know through what you see and feel. Its epistemology begins and largely ends in the viscera. As blasphemous as it may appear to say it, television has something of the power we associate with religious communication, at least in the sense that it relies heavily on moral teachings resting on an emotional base.

These differences in the form in which each curriculum codifies its information—the difference between pictures and words, analogic and digital symbols, narrative and expositional styles, parables and arguments—certainly account for the fact that the school curriculum is hierarchical, rigidly graded, and based on the principle of the prerequisite, whereas the TV curriculum is almost totally undifferentiated. Concepts, generalizations, verbal knowledge—reasoning itself—are hierarchical in nature. There is a structure to ideas. They are built one upon another, and you must be able to comprehend lower orders of concepts before comprehending those of greater complexity. That is almost the whole reason for prerequisites in school.

But I doubt if there is a hierarchy either of imagery or feeling. Or, if there is, it is of such subtlety that no one has yet been able to organize it into graded levels. In any case, the TV curriculum has not found it necessary to do so. It presents its subject matter whole, without regard to age, sex, level of maturity, or education. There are no prerequisites for watching television—not for watching *Laverne and Shirley* or for watching Jacques Cousteau. This gives to the TV curriculum a sense of completeness which cannot exist in a curriculum based on orders of complexity. In the school curriculum, there is always more to know, another concept or refinement of a skill to be learned. In the TV curriculum, one knows, or at least feels, everything at once. This is one reason why you can miss one or several of Professor Gabe Kaplan's lessons without having anything to "make up." But if you miss one of Professor Postman's lessons, you fall behind. In the TV curriculum, there is no such thing as "falling behind." All lessons are on the same plane. There is nothing to be retarded and nothing to be developed.

This fact is one of the sources of TV's enormous capacity to satisfy. Within the TV curriculum there is no deferred gratification. Perhaps the most powerful bias of television is, in fact, its stress on immediate gratification, for television has no need to put its learners on "hold" with a view toward later intellectual or emotional satisfaction. TV does not require you either to remember or anticipate anything. One may go so far as to say that the TV curriculum has achieved, in an unexpected and upside-down way, what so many educators have always hoped for, a hope expressed in the phrase "learning for its own sake." Whereas the school curriculum promises future intellectual rewards for learning its lessons, the TV curriculum promises no rewards whatsoever. *Attending to it is its own reward.* In a nonhierarchical, analogic information system based on immediate emotional response, there is no future, or sense of continuity, or need for preparation. The pleasure of total comprehension and involvement is immediately accessible. The Kingdom of God is of this world, now, and not of any other, later.

This dimension of immediacy is reinforced in many ways on television, particularly in the length of its lessons. The learning modules of the TV curriculum are extremely short and compact—commercials run anywhere from ten to sixty seconds; what are called "programs" run from thirty to sixty minutes but are always sequenced in eight- to ten-minute modules. The commercials are an especially important component of the TV curriculum because between the ages of five and eighteen, a youngster will see approximately 675,000 commercials, at the rate of about 1000 per week. This makes the television commercial the most voluminous information source in the education of youth. And this means that we can assume that our youth are being conditioned to intense concentration for short periods of time, and deconditioned, so to speak, to sustained concentration. Moreover, it is important to say that television commercials, which are subject to easy ridicule by those who know little about information environments, are almost never about anything trivial, especially from the point of view of youth. Mouthwash commercials are not about bad breath. They are about the need for social acceptance and, frequently, about the need to be sexually attractive. Beer commercials are almost always about the need to share the values of a peer group. An automobile commercial may be about one's need for autonomy or social status; a toilet paper commercial about one's fear of nature. Television commercials are about products only in the sense that the story of Jonah is about the anatomy of whales. To miss this point is to miss much of what the television curriculum sets out to do, for, especially in commercials, it is concerned to teach, by parable, that serious human worries are resolvable through relatively simple means and that, therefore, the resolution of anything problematic is never far away. You will note, I'm sure, that this teaching is almost the exact opposite of what schools are accustomed to assume about the nature and resolution of human problems.

In fact, the TV curriculum contradicts in another, hardly subtle way what traditional schools have always assumed. It is an axiomatic part of scholarship that all things have consequences and that our history is never irrelevant to our present or future. Even our traditional theology teaches that. We may overcome, or reproach, our history but we cannot deny its existence. But it is in the nature of TV's imagistic, present-oriented, time-compressed curriculum to be nonsequential; that is, discontinuous. There is almost nothing on television, however high its quality, that has anything to do with anything else on television. Here, for example, is a slice of the TV syllabus for one day, selected at random, which is the only way it can be selected:

The Waltons—Ben leaves Walton's Mountain after losing his part-time job, and his hopes of becoming a full-time employee at Jarvis's used car lot.

Welcome Back, Kotter—"Epstein's Term Paper." Epstein's plan for a passing grade backfires when Mr. Kotter discovers a similarity between the student's term paper and one he submitted himself ten years earlier.

Masterpiece Theatre—"I, Claudius: Fool's Luck." Claudius proves to be a Solomon rather than an idiot, beginning his reign with peace and prosperity.

Class of '65—"The Class Beauty." Despite her mother's ambitions for her, Wendy Sparks, the class beauty, maintains a cold and aloof attitude toward men.

The Odd Couple—Dressed in bizarre costumes, Felix, Oscar, and Nancy find themselves locked inside their apartment basement.

You will note, first, the quasi-religious nature of the content of some of these programs. As I said earlier, most television programs are suffused with moral lessons. In this, they cannot help themselves since stories must inevitably take a point of view about how people should behave themselves.

The question of what sort of religious teaching this is will be addressed in a wider context in the next chapter. Here, I am mainly interested in showing that there is an almost overwhelming sense of incoherence to the TV curriculum. A school curriculum, even one that has not been well thought out, always tries to proceed from some organizing principle. It may be based on a hierarchy of concepts, as in mathematics. Or it may move chronologically from one point to another, as in history. Or it may be held together by some theme, as in literature. In television, however, there is no organizing principle. There is no chronology, or theme, or logical sequence. The world to which television is the window is presented as fragmented, unorganizable, without structure of any kind. Even to the extent that TV, in some sense, puts forward a theology, it is a theology without a moral center, without historical precedents, without general application. What does Epstein have to do with Claudius? Or Claudius with the Class of '65? And what do the dilemmas of Oscar and Felix have to do with Ben Walton's losing his job? And what do the commercials that come in between these programs have to do with what comes before or goes after? For that matter, what does today's news as presented on television have to do with yesterday's news? And what is the connection between a Toyota commercial and an earthquake in Chile?

The answer to all these questions is, "Nothing." Perhaps the most coherent content of the entire TV curriculum is a five-day weather forecast in which one is shown what a rainstorm in Texas on Monday has to do with a snowstorm in New York on Friday. The rest of the content consists of discrete and isolated events, images, and stories which have no implications very far beyond themselves and which certainly have no continuity. Whereas the content of school may be likened at least in principle to a play in which there is a beginning, middle, and end, the content of TV is like a vaudeville show in which there are only acts. They are replaceable and reversible, having no relationship to each other. But it is a vaudeville show without an end, for the TV curriculum is almost always at hand and runs continuously. You are not excused from it for summer vacation, illness, weekends, or Christmas holidays. And, in some places, it operates around the clock. Thus, it is able to integrate itself into the student's life in a way that the school curriculum can never approach. Moreover, the TV curriculum is almost always experienced at home. There is no reason for it to assign homework. It is by its nature *home* work. And this fact leads to a striking paradox.

Whereas the school curriculum is community-centered— that is, learning takes place in the presence of others in something approximating a ritualized context—the TV curriculum is individual-centered. One might say that it is the ultimate example of individualized instruction, although not in the sense that the lessons are designed for particular individuals, but rather in the sense that individuals learn in isolation. All the other TV students are invisible to the learner, and cannot intrude either their defects or virtues on his concentration. The paradox lies in the fact that television is customarily thought of as a mass medium. But in one sense it is far less so than the school. For school is, if nothing else, a communal situation, a medium that demands a public gathering. Television is an individualizing medium. One experiences TV and responds to it in psychological as well as physical isolation from others. School teaches you to behave as a member of a group. Television teaches you to behave as an individual. In school, an individual is continuously required to modify his or her behavior to conform to the aims and needs of the group. To misbehave in school means, for the most part, to violate a group norm. But in attending to the TV curriculum, one may exhibit almost any kind of behavior. One is free to eat, do homework, knit, lie down,

stand up, talk, read a magazine—do whatever seems to satisfy one's own aims and needs.

Moreover, the bias toward individualistic response is enhanced by the "elective" nature of the TV curriculum. The
learner can choose whatever lesson pleases him or her. There
are no required courses. No major or minor subjects. One
can drop any course in a second when interest wanes. A turn
of the wrist is one's "drop-add" slip. No group responsibility
or consultation is required.

In respect to TV's individualizing bias, the effects of TV
would appear, at first thought, to duplicate the effects of the
printed book when it first intruded itself into Western culture. As Harold Innis has postulated, the book, which demands privacy and encourages individual choice and response, had the effect of splitting the individual off from a
group learning context and thereby generated an irresistible
urge to individualism. But this similarity between television
and the book is, I believe, entirely superficial. In the first
place, the book entered societies that were predominantly
community-centered. It served a thermostatic function in
that it promoted individualism within the context of societies
organized around and devoted to its opposite. In the case of
America, television has entered a society already greatly
committed to individualism. Thus, it is quite possible that by
vastly increasing isolated learning, television encourages
only idiosyncracy and the attractions of anarchy.

Second, because books, even bad ones, are ultimately
about ideas, they have the effect of encouraging the individualism of independent and critical thought. Books, as David
Riesman once said, act as a kind of gunpowder of the mind.
In this, they can scarcely help themselves, for English sentences organized in linear sequence on a page have almost no
interest beyond what they symbolize. They are not especially
lovely to look at. They do not move around and dazzle the
eye. There is in fact nothing for them to do but to invite

attention to their meaning, which in turn generates criticism of their meaning, and then the construction of alternatives to their meaning. But this is not true for television. The TV image offers interesting and dynamic form, not interesting and dynamic ideational content. That is why viewers can watch the same program five and six times without boredom, for even the stories themselves are subordinate to the attractions of the individual image. One is drawn by the fascination of these images, especially images of personalities who are familiar. Even the content of TV news programs is almost wholly irrelevant to the viewer. Except in rare instances, we watch to see the teller of the news, not to hear what he tells. And this is why Ralph Nader can appear on *Saturday Night Live* or Richard Nixon on *Laugh-In* without one's experiencing an acute case of incongruity. What they have to say is of no importance on TV. It is their image, not their words, to which we attend. Who would really be surprised if Anwar el-Sadat made a guest appearance on *The Little House on the Prairie*? What difference would it make anyway? We expect very few connections between the imagery of television and the world of ideas and issues. In a medium in which the image captures most attention, personality supercedes—in fact, all but obliterates—ideas and issues. That is why one becomes a celebrity by the mere fact of appearing on television. No prior accomplishment is required. Nor a reason for being there. It is accomplishment enough for one's image to be on television. It is its own reason. In such a situation, individualism takes on a wholly different aspect from its meaning in a book culture. The individualism of the book leads to the dominance of the mind. The individualism of TV leads to the dominance of personality.

There are two other characteristics of the TV curriculum which bear mentioning because they are in sharp contrast with the school curriculum. They are also in sharp contrast with each other, which makes them especially interesting. The first is that the TV curriculum is largely authoritarian, which is to say that its information moves in one direction. There is no way that television students can modify or control the speed, pace, form, quantity, content, or anything else of their lessons. No questions may be addressed to their instructor. No complaints may be lodged. No special arrangements can be requested. Even the "elective" nature of the TV curriculum, alluded to before, does not mitigate the absence of any feedback possibilities. To be sure, a student can turn off a lesson—let us say, *Happy Days*—and turn to another more to his liking—say, *Baretta*—but he remains entirely impotent to affect either the structure or content of the lesson.

School, of course, is not famous for its democratic structure. But even the harshest school critic will concede that the classroom is by no means a unidirectional system. If nothing else, misbehavior itself is a form of feedback, and no teacher can be indifferent to it. But except in the rarest instances (and I have personally never seen one), a teacher will permit questions, will ask for and even demand responses, will repeat and review according to need, will encourage students to exert influence on their lessons. Even when a teacher is asking "What-Am-I-Thinking" types of questions, the point is to produce *output* from students. Output is not possible in the TV curriculum, at least not in the sense I mean it here. The TV curriculum provides only input, and this fact, incidentally, may have something to do with the increase in student misbehavior in school. When people are denied access to routes of response in one information system, they will frequently be outrageously expressive when they find themselves in a situation where response is both possible and permissible. The school curriculum, then, for all of its legendary demands for obedience and passivity, is far less authoritarian than the TV curriculum. It has, at least, an audience, meaning people who are capable of acting on the environment. TV, in this sense, has no audience.

At the same time, while the school curriculum tries to distribute knowledge in an orderly and authoritative way, the TV curriculum continuously undermines authority. Television is both authoritarian and contemptuous of authority at the same time. As Harold Innis points out, every new medium has the capability of breaking up "knowledge monopolies." The phonetic alphabet broke the knowledge monopoly of the priests whose secrets were codified in complex ideographs. The printing press broke the knowledge monopoly of those few writers and readers who controlled the manuscript culture. Television attacks the monopoly of the printed word. In fact, by distributing information, albeit in pictures, to everyone in the culture simultaneously, it threatens all systems that have a hierarchical structure. A hierarchy is a drama played by superiors, inferiors, and equals. Information is the means by which we assign people their role in the drama and, indeed, justify that role. In principle, those at the top have more information and more access to information than those at the bottom. That is essentially why they are at the top and the others at the bottom. Moreover, every hierarchy has a certain pattern of distributing information. For example, you cannot get into medical school until you have been to college, and to college until you have been to high school. This is what is called "prerequisites," to which I have alluded before. The concept of a prerequisite is based on the metaphor of constructing a building. The earliest information you get will provide the foundation. Then, in an orderly, sequential way, you will, by acquiring a measured and predetermined amount of information, move yourself toward the top floor. This is an entirely rational way of proceeding—it is certainly the way of the school —except when there is a television antenna on the roof. Television is the enemy of foundations and prerequisites, and therefore hostile to the basis of traditional authority. TV turns hierarchies on their sides. By conveying information in nonhierarchical distribution patterns, it creates a deeply felt impression that there is no rational reason for tops and bottoms, or for secrets, or for knowledge monopolies. In such a situation everyone goes into business for himself. Or believes that he ought to. We move toward a culture of political, spiritual, and social entrepreneurs. It could be very dangerous, especially when the means by which traditional authority is undermined is, itself, exceedingly authoritarian.

Now, you may have the impression from what I have just said, as well as from all that preceded it, that I strongly disapprove of the TV curriculum. But this is in fact not the case, and is also beside the point. TV will not go away, and in all likelihood will continue to increase its influence and prestige in our information environment. It is pointless to spend time or energy deploring television, or even making proposals to "improve" it. Of course, the seriousness, maturity, and general quality of the content of its programs certainly can be increased. But the characteristics I am talking about are deeply embedded in the structure of television. They are an integral part of the *environment* that television creates. From this point of view, television cannot be improved.

As I have described it, the TV curriculum has the following characteristics: It is

> *attention-centered*
>
> *nonpunitive*
>
> *affect-centered*
>
> *present-centered*
>
> *image-centered*
>
> *narration-centered*

moralistic

nonanalytical

nonhierarchical

authoritarian

contemptuous of authority

continuous in time

isolating in space

discontinuous in content

immediately and intrinsically gratifying

No amount of academic complaints or "responsible" calls for TV reform can change any of the above. TV is not a school, or a book, or any curriculum other than itself. It does what its structure makes it do, and it teaches as it must. The real pragmatic issue is not TV but its relationship to other systematic teachings in the information environment. The question is, To what extent can the biases of TV be balanced by the biases of other information systems, particularly the school? But before we get to that, we must yet consider, in some careful way, what are likely to be the consequences of an unchallenged television education. What will its biases lead to? Without considering that, we cannot know what sorts of defenses to prepare.

4
The Teachings of the Media Curriculum

Since the television curriculum is pervasive and powerful, we can assume that it will have effects at several levels, including the physiological, the psychological, and the social. Of the physiological, we can, of course, only make conjectures. Nothing will really be known for a very long time, and not by us. But it can reasonably be imagined that excessive immersion in nonlinguistic, analogic symbols will have the effect of amplifying the functions of the right hemisphere of the brain while inhibiting the functions of the left. The left hemisphere is the source of most of our language power (at least for righthanded people). A left hemisphere lesion will lead to damage to our capacity to speak, write, count, compute, and reason (but not necessarily to our capacity to sing, a fact which might have been suspected by Plato had he been a brain surgeon). The right hemisphere of the brain is largely nonlinguistic and nonlogical in both its coding and decoding of information. Such language as it is capable of is underdeveloped and lacks both the syntax and semantics required for digital communication. Apparently, the right brain works through pattern recognition, which is to say it apprehends the world holistically rather than through linguistic structures. In recognizing a human face, or a picture of it, or anything that requires an "all at once" perception, such as watching TV, we are largely using the right hemisphere of the brain, the left possibly being something of a burden in the process. Thus, continuous TV watching over centuries could conceivably have the effect of weakening left-brain activity, and producing a population of "right-brained" people.[1]

What this would mean is difficult to say except that we may guess that such people would be strong on intuition and feeling but weak on reflection and analysis. The left hemisphere, being the source of our power to speak and, therefore, to categorize, name, and objectify experience, has apparently been in the ascendancy for several millennia of human development. A good case can be made, along the lines Julian Jaynes has pursued, that the gradual emergence of left-brain dominance has generated our uniquely human capacity for consciousness; that is, our capacity to reconstruct the past and project ourselves into a future.[2] A reversal of this trend is certainly imaginable as the word recedes in importance and the fast-moving, analogic image replaces it. If we imagine such a reverse trend carried to an extreme over many centuries, we might, then, have people who are "in touch with their feelings," who are spontaneous and musical, and who live in an existential world of immediate experience but who, at the same time, cannot "think" in the way we customarily use that word. In other words, people whose state of mind is somewhat analogous to that of a modern-day baboon.

But one does not need to resort to millennia-wide speculation about the modification of brain functions in order to talk about the consequences of an unopposed TV education. There are, even now, observable behaviors in our youth that indicate they are undergoing certain serious psychological changes, at least in part attributable to television. For example, I have already suggested that the highly compressed TV learning modules, especially those of ten- to thirty-second commercials, are affecting attention span. Many teachers have commented on the fact that students, of all ages, "turn off" when some lesson or lecture takes longer than, say, eight to ten minutes. TV conditioning leads to the expectation that there will be a new point of view or focus of interest or even subject matter every few minutes, and it is becoming increasingly difficult for the young to sustain attention in situations where there is a fixed point of view or an extended linear progression.

There is also evidence that youth are exhibiting behaviors —for example, in school—that are appropriate to TV watching but not to situations requiring group attention. For instance, it is not uncommon for teachers to report that students will openly read newspapers in class or engage in other unconcealed side-involvements which are usually considered to be "rude" in the context of a lesson or lecture. My own investigation of this phenomenon suggests that these behaviors are not "rude" if we mean by that word a deliberate effort to violate the rules of a social situation. Many students are not aware that they have violated any rule at all. In watching television, or listening to records or the radio, they continuously engage in such side-involvements without reproach, and do not always understand why these behaviors are inappropriate when carried over to other communication environments.

It has, of course, also been widely noticed that the linguistic powers of our youth appear to be diminishing. Scores on reading tests are in decline. But even more important, writing, which is the clearest demonstration of the power of analytical and sequential thinking, seems increasingly to be an alien form to many of our young, even to those who may be regarded as extremely intelligent. Moreover, it has been observed that oral expression has not improved as writing skills have fallen off. There are many teachers, for example, who have abandoned giving writing assignments altogether but who have not found their students to be especially organized or even coherent in talking about anything of minimal complexity.

What makes this deficiency especially alarming is that it suggests we are, in fact, not moving back to a pre-Platonic oral culture in which memory, argumentation, and dialectic take command. Astonishingly, the two electronic media which are perfectly suited to the transmission of the human voice—the radio and phonograph—have been given over almost entirely to the transmission of music. Such language as is heard on records is little else but comedy routines, or song lyrics at the level of Neanderthal chanting. On radio, language is largely a commercial message, mostly a parody of human speech—disjointed, semihysterical, almost completely devoid of ideational content.

I believe this development to be only in part a consequence of the economic structure of the broadcasting and record industries. For if we say that these industries only give our youth what they will pay for, the question remains, Why do our youth turn away from civilized speech? The answer, in my opinion, is that the electronic information environment, with television at its center, is fundamentally hostile to conceptual, segmented, linear modes of expression, so that both writing and speech must lose some of their power. Language is, by its nature, slow moving, hierarchical, logical, and continuous. Whether writing or speaking, one must maintain a fixed point of view and a continuity of content; one must move to higher or lower levels of abstraction; one must follow to a greater or lesser degree rules of syntax and logic. Even more, language is inevitably ambiguous. As Chaim Perelman says it, language is filled with confused notions. It is this very ambiguity that gives natural language its conceptual scope and versatility. For every word contains the possibility of multiple meanings and therefore of multiple ideas. And because words do not have closed, invariant meanings, they are our most effective instruments for changing our concepts and making them grow. The word is not just an idea. It is a small universe of ideas. Even further, every spoken sentence contains the seed of an argument, not only because of its ambiguity but because whatever is asserted simultaneously implies its negation or opposite. Every proposition is debatable or at least an impetus to inquiry.

But the television curriculum will have none of this. Or, at least, very little. As I have argued, its imagery is fast moving, concrete, discontinuous, alogical, requiring emotional response, not conceptual processing. Not being propositional in form, its imagery does not provide grounds for argument and contains little ambiguity. There is nothing to debate about. Nothing to refute. Nothing to negate. There are only feelings to be felt. Thus the TV curriculum poses a serious challenge not merely to school performance but to civilization itself. And the challenge is not made only by the TV curriculum, for in considering what we are facing we must take into account the cumulative impact of the entire electronic information environment of which TV is only an element, although a central one. Radio, the LP record, audio-tape, the photograph, and film, each in its own way lends support to the undermining of traditional patterns of thought and response. Taken together, their "hidden curriculum" conspires against almost all of the assumptions on which the slowly disseminated, logically ordered, and cognitively processed word is based. In an environment in which nonlinguistic information is moved at the speed of light, in nonhierarchical patterns, in vast and probably unassimilable quantities, the word and all it stands for must lose prestige, power, and relevance.

Our problem, then, is not how to produce higher reading

scores or better school compositions but how to close the "generation gap." "Generation gap" means here that on one side there stands the age-old tradition of a language-centered view of the world, and on the other there stands a recently emerged image-centered view. On one side, therefore, there is always an historical presence with its mirror image, the future. On the other there is only an overpowering present. On one side there is the ideal of reason; on the other there is the ideal of authenticity of feeling.

Do I overstate the case? I certainly hope so. And yet the effects to which I am alluding can be observed not simply in the fragmented, impatient speech of the young or their illogical, unsyntactical writing but in the rapid emergence of an all-instant society: instant therapy, instant religion, instant food, instant friends, even instant reading. Instancy is one of the main teachings of our present information environment. Constancy is one of the main teachings of civilization. But constancy presupposes the relevance of historical precedence, of continuity, and above all, of complexity and the richness of ambiguity. A person trained to read a page in three seconds is being taught contempt for complexity and ambiguity. A person trained to restructure his or her life in a weekend of therapy is being taught not only contempt for complexity and ambiguity but for the meaning of one's own past. And a person who abandons a five-thousand- or two-thousand-year-old religious tradition to follow a fourteen-year-old messenger from God has somehow learned to value novelty more than continuity.

Where does the seeming plausibility of instancy as a way of life come from? It is at least a reasonable hypothesis that it emerges from the "world view" advanced by our present information environment. Consider this: Every one of the one million commercials—every one—that a youngster will see or hear on TV or the radio presents a problem and a solution. The problem, as I have noted, is rarely trivial but the solution always is. Your anxiety about your sexual appeal gets solved with Scope—in thirty seconds. Your failure to achieve social status gets solved with a bottle of Coke and a song—in sixty seconds. Your fear of nature gets solved with Scott toilet tissue—in twenty seconds. Even the heartbreak of psoriasis can be relieved in a few seconds, not to mention the agony of hemorrhoidal tissues or, through Pan Am, the boredom of your life. These are powerful and incessant teachings, which are not only directed at the young. They present us all with a paradigm of how to think and how to live and what to expect. We become, as Edmund Carpenter says, what we behold. The new media are more than extensions of our senses. They are ultimately metaphors for life itself, directing us to search for time-compressed experience, short-term relationships, present-oriented accomplishment, simple and immediate solutions. Thus, the teaching of the media curriculum must lead inevitably to a disbelief in long-term planning, in deferred gratification, in the relevance of tradition, and in the need for confronting complexity.

But this is far from the end of it. There are many reasonable hypotheses about the teachings of our electronic information environment for which there exists suggestive evidence and against which civilization must prepare itself. For example, the nonlinear, nonsequential nature of electronic information works in powerful ways to create a frame of mind hostile to science. Science depends on linearity of thought, the step-by-step presentation of evidence and argumentation. This method of organizing information is the structural basis of scientific thought. It makes possible the refutation of evidence and argument; it permits translation into other digital forms, such as mathematics; it encourages delayed response and reflective analysis. The growth of science also depends on our ability to create increasingly sophisticated abstractions, particularly in digital modes. What happens, then, if our information environment does not encourage this mode of thinking? It is improbable that scientists will disappear but we shall quite likely have fewer of them, and they are likely to form, even in the short run, an elite class who, like priests of the pictographic age, will be believed to possess mystical powers. The rest of the population may move rapidly toward an increasing fascination with mysticism and superstition; in other words, beliefs which are neither refutable or comprehensible but which are expressed with great feeling. There is already some evidence that this is in fact happening, as we can see in the growth of interest and belief in the occult, astrology, Eastern mysticism, levitating gurus, and English-speaking extraterrestrials.

Scientific thinking must also recede in prestige and relevance because of the discontinuity of content that characterizes much of our information environment. The fundamental assumption of science is that there is order and unity in diversity. A scientist must believe that events can be explained by reference to some organizing principle. Above all, he must believe the world *makes sense*. But when one is immersed in a world of disconnected media presentations, it is extremely difficult to internalize this assumption. The young in particular are experiencing an acute inability to make connections, and some have given up trying. The TV curriculum, we must remember, stresses the fragmented and discrete nature of events, and indeed is structurally unable to organize them into coherent themes or principles.

This fact must inevitably contribute to the undermining of a sense of history, as well. Like science, history requires a belief in connectedness—the assumption that there are explanatory principles which account for social change or human conflict or intellectual growth. In this context, Jacob Bronowski's *The Ascent of Man* offers an instructive case of the nature of our problem, for it is about both history and science. Although the book version of his ideas was, in fact, a television script, it has the power, because it is a book, to explain the principles by which culture and science have developed; that is, the book has a thesis. In the TV version, the thesis disappeared. And so did history. Television is always in the present tense. There is no way to show what happened in the past. Whatever is shown appears as something that *is* happening. This is why we must be told frequently that a videotape we are watching was actually recorded at some earlier date. But even when film is used, as was the case in Bronowski's programs, it must present history as "now." In the "grammar" of both film and TV, there simply is no correlate to a linguistic past tense. So, much of Bronowski's point of view was lost. He was concerned to show historical development but the audience saw only a series of interesting events of equivalent contemporaneousness. Moreover, TV or film cannot reveal a thesis. A thesis, a principle, a theme, a law, a hypothesis—these are all linguistic concepts. Pictures have no theses. They are analogues whose level of abstraction is concrete and invariable, and whose impact is immediate and existential. While Bronowski *talked* his thesis as a supplement to the images, his talk could not compete with his pictures. In the end, what the audience saw was a series of discrete, disconnected images which had no history and suggested no principles.

We must also worry about the plausible hypothesis that any decline in linguistic power will tend to increase the extent of personal maladjustment. As I write, there are reports from colleges and universities all over the country about the widespread incidence of suicide and other less definitive but serious symptoms of emotional difficulty among youth.[3] We appear to have an epidemic on our hands. Without meaning to deprecate the usefulness of either art or music therapy, I think it accurate to say that articulate language is our chief weapon against mental disturbance. Through language we are able to formulate in relatively clear terms the origins and nature of our distress, and through language we may chart the route toward resolution and relief. I seriously doubt if you can sing, dance, draw, or scream your way out of an impulse to suicide. But you can talk your way out. Of course, you can talk your way in, as well, which is why knowledge of and competence in language are so essential to helping one achieve and maintain emotional balance. I have already written one book on this subject, *Crazy Talk, Stupid Talk,* and do not intend to rewrite it here. But surely it is no startling thesis to say that any decline in the resources of language is likely to be accompanied by an increase in personal maladjustment or, if you will, crazy talk.

And when we put the nonlinguistic bias of the media together with their bias toward one-way communication, the result is something more than maladjustment symptoms. We may have a near-lethal problem in social psychology. For example, there is no doubt that the new information environment provides access to knowledge about events and people all over the world. Through electronic media everyone's affairs become our business. The phrase Marshall McLuhan has used to describe this situation is "the world as global village." But if we all live in a global village, it is a strange village indeed: though we live in it, we are both mute and powerless. In fact, we do not live in it. We observe it, and can exert no influence upon it. Even worse, we cannot even decide what portions of the village or aspects of its life we will see, or the points of view from which we will see it. These decisions are made by the frame of a television screen, by the values of a television director, according to the biases of a television network.

What is the effect of making people aware of many things over which they have no control? I would suspect that it leads to anomie and an increasing sense of impotence. There are occasions, such as during the Viet Nam War, when a large segment of the population is capable of rousing itself and responding to a grievance. There have been other occasions when similar mass responses have occurred. But the point is that these responses must be made en masse. Individuals no longer live in a context which allows them to have an impact on their environment. McLuhan himself has described the problem. "When man lives in an electric environment," he says, "his nature is transformed and his private identity is merged with a corporate whole. He becomes 'Mass Man.' Mass man is a phenomenon of electric speed, not of physical quantity. Mass man was first noticed as a phenomenon in the age of radio, but he had come into existence, unnoticed, with the electric telegraph."[4]

Mass man, as we know, can be an exceedingly dangerous animal, especially in a situation where there exists skepticism about the basis of traditional authority.[5] As I have pointed out, the electronic information environment tends to undermine hierarchies, while television in particular amplifies the appeal of personality. In such an environment, totalitarian ideas expressed by charismatic people find a congenial ground for growth. It is no accident that Reverend Moon, Werner Erhard, L. Ron Hubbard, and other messiahs with expensive tastes are especially appealing to the young.

But the undermining of hierarchies through the rapid and undifferentiated diffusion of information contains the possibility of still other undesirable consequences. I have already referred to the fact that hierarchies always involve "secrets." There are, of course, many kinds of secrets, including information that everyone knows but which is not considered suitable for public sharing. Everyone knows, for example, what one does in the bathroom but it is part of our concept of personal dignity and civilized interaction that we do not display it or discuss it. What is shared between a priest and a sinner, what happens among members of a family, what is discussed between a psychiatrist and a patient, these are secrets, too. Or used to be, for the electronic environment assists in the dissolution of secrets.[6]

In the first place, some of the social structures—for example, the family and church—which are traditionally places and occasions for secret-sharing have diminished in prestige and influence. Thus, people turn to strangers, that is, public forums, including electronic forums, to reveal their secrets. The emergence of the radio phone-in show is explainable, in part, by this need. It is a form of controlled exhibitionism, and is thus both a symptom and cause of the blurring of the difference between private life and public life. As Richard Sennett suggests in *The Fall of Public Man*, electronic communication is one means by which the distinction between private and public life is brought to an end.

But more important, the new media require a constant supply of information. Television, for example, is compelled to display novel events continuously in order to control the public's attention. Thus, any sphere of human activity is a potential source of supply. We have already seen the Loud family display every conceivable secret of their private life, a president and his wife being asked to discuss their bedroom habits, a host of a daytime TV program being analyzed by his psychiatrist, babies getting born, transvestites discussing their sex-change operations, and so on. So far as I know, there has not yet been a program in which moral transgressors confess their sins to priests, or physicians tell patients they are going to die. But in principle there is no reason why we shall not have them. Television and radio (and one might add, the movies) are inherently hostile to the *idea* of privacy. But it is a hostility without vindictiveness or even emotion. There is certainly nothing conspiratorial about it. Simply, information must be moved and consumed continuously. That is the price to be paid for speed-of-light transmission. What the information may be is of no consequence, as long as it is attention-getting, and does not inhibit the flow of new information coming fast behind it. Of course, in the process, our ideas of propriety and personal identity become altered;

that is to say, dangerously eroded. The Mass Man, as McLuhan describes him, is one whose private identity is merged with the corporate whole. What this means, as Bruno Bettelheim has described it in *The Informed Heart,* is that people are stripped of their secrets and therefore of their sense of personal dignity. The relatively new "values" of openness, of letting it all hang out, of not being uptight, of saying exactly what is on your mind, are a consequence of the present information environment. We are being moved rapidly away from the concept of a private identity by the egalitarianism of total, undifferentiated information disclosure.

There is still another consequence of this movement, described very well by C. P. Snow. He observed in 1968 at Westminster College that ". . . the rapidity and completeness of human communications are constantly presenting us with the sight of famine, suffering, violent death. We turn away, inside our safe drawing rooms. It may be that these communications themselves help to make us callous." You will recognize in this conjecture the conventional complaint against the display of excessive violence, for example on TV. It is not a complaint to be taken lightly. But there is another meaning to callousness here that is, in my opinion, even more ominous. I refer to a certain degree of immunization and therefore indifference to reality itself that may be generated by the "rapidity and completeness of human communications." That is, even if there were a reduction in the images of famine, suffering, and violent death, there would be no reduction in the amount of *symbolic* experience in which we are daily immersed. Again, what is important here is not so much the content of the media but the experience of media itself. Life on the TV screen, however it is depicted, is still seen through a twenty-one-inch flat-surfaced frame. Life on the movie screen is seen seven times life size. Even when we hear an authentic human voice on the radio, it is a voice entirely disembodied. Life, then, becomes a stylized, edited media event, and it is not inconceivable that in the "completeness" of our immersion in media, we come to prefer media-life to reality itself.

Even before the electronic revolution we understood the role that reading itself may play in encouraging a fantasy life. There were probably many readers in the nineteenth century, for example, who preferred fictional characters and places to the real people and situations they were forced to live with. If we now multiply by a factor of ten the opportunities for experiencing life at a distance, life through the filter of a technological symbolic system, we can get some idea of the extent to which media may now be serving as a surrogate for reality, and a preferred one at that. At stadiums throughout the country, huge TV screens have been installed so that spectators can experience the game through TV because TV is better than being there, even when you are there. Conferences and other group meetings are videotaped so that participants may look at themselves to see what "really happened." Tourists travel everywhere with still cameras so that they can document their vacations. In the end, the photographs are the reality of the experience. Should they be ruined, how would one know what was really seen? Or if one was really there? And we must remember that not only did "Marcus Welby" receive more than a quarter of a million letters seeking his medical advice but that the American Medical Association actually invited him to be a keynote speaker at one of their annual conventions. Perhaps it is not even too much to say that the increase in what are called "senseless" crimes is part of the consequence of the replacement of reality with symbolic experience. For the "sense" in "senseless" has two meanings, one of which refers to thinking, the other to touch, smell, taste, and so on. Is it possible that a "senseless" crime has its origin in an acute deprivation of real sensory experience? Is it possible that, immersed in a world of surrogate experience, we both lose our senses and lose touch with them at the same time?

Admittedly, this last observation, as well as some that preceded it, must be regarded as speculation. But none of it is "mere" speculation. I believe that reason, historical analogy, and observable trends within our society point to their plausibility. We can be sure that a curriculum as powerful as the electronic information environment will have powerful effects, and in suggesting what these might be, I have done nothing more than what educators do every September when they predict the effects of a school curriculum. They tell us that certain things will be taught in certain ways, within a certain context, and that there are certain results that can be expected. I am saying the same thing, with this difference: The curriculum I am referring to has more money spent on it, commands greater attention, is more pervasive, and is less carefully monitored than the school curriculum. Moreover, in its competition with the school curriculum for the control of our young, the electronic curriculum is an ungracious— one might even say, merciless—adversary. It makes no concessions whatsoever to the school curriculum, unless you want to count *Sesame Street,* which is, in my opinion, no concession at all but a promiscuous flaunting of everything the TV curriculum represents and the school curriculum does not. The school curriculum, on the other hand, yields at almost every point and in the worst possible way—by trying to mimic the forms of the electronic curriculum and therefore to indulge its biases. School courses are reduced to twenty-minute modules so that children's attention will not wander. Required courses are eliminated and replaced with inconsequential electives. Teachers become entertainers. Programmed machines and other techniques which stress isolated learning are introduced. Audio-visual aids flood the classroom. Relevant—that is, attention-centered—topics are stressed. There even develops a widespread interest in what are called "alternative curriculums." But the school as we normally think of it (or used to think of it) is now, itself, an alternative curriculum, one whose teachings very much need to be preserved in the face of the onslaught of the First Curriculum.

The school curriculum is subject-matter-centered, word-centered, reason-centered, future-centered, hierarchical, secular, socializing, segmented, and coherent. Assuming that these characteristics are maintained, and even strengthened, we may hope that the education of our youth will achieve a healthful balance, and therefore a survival-insuring direction. Marshall McLuhan wrote prophetically more than a decade ago that our education must assume a thermostatic function. He said: "Just as we now try to control atom-bomb fallout, so we will one day try to control media fallout. Education will become recognized as civil defense against media fallout."[7]

In Section III of this book I hope to show exactly how this might be done. But there are still some other problems that need to be acknowledged and discussed before moving to solutions. And one of them is the Technical Thesis.

5
The Technical Thesis

Every once in a while an archeologist will discover an artifact which captures perfectly the ethos of some past age. Or more precisely, reveals the nature of its most burdensome disease. I believe I have come across such an artifact, one that will tell future archeologists, in capsule form, exactly what we have had to endure in our own age. The artifact is an advertisement which tells of a machine called HAGOTH. Anyone can buy it for fifteen hundred dollars, making it one of the best bargains of this decade. HAGOTH has sixteen lights—eight green and eight red. If you connect HAGOTH to your telephone, you are able to tell whether or not someone talking to you is telling the truth.[1]

The way it does this is by analyzing the "stress" content of a human voice. You ask your telephone caller some key questions, and HAGOTH will go to work in analyzing his replies. Red lights go on when there is much stress in his voice, green when there is little. As the ad says, "Green indicates no stress, hence truthfulness." Red means you are being deceived. It is really quite like magic. HAGOTH, in other words, works exactly like an IQ test. In an IQ test, you connect a pencil to the fingers of a youth, address some key questions to him, and from his replies you can tell exactly how intelligent he is. There is a margin of error, of course, as there is in HAGOTH, but in the main the machinery of both HAGOTH and an IQ test is trusted by our citizenry: It gives us the sort of information we value in a form we respect.

There are several reasons why this is so. The first is that the machines themselves define what they measure. HAGOTH defines "stress" and thereby "truthfulness" and "deception" by the extent of the oscillations in a voice. Therefore, since (one assumes) it accurately measures oscillations, HAGOTH can't be wrong. It is a self-confirming system. An IQ test defines intelligence as what it measures. Therefore, your score is by definition a precise reflection of your intelligence. Simply, both HAGOTH and an IQ test define what they measure, then measure their definition. In this way we achieve clarity.

Second, both HAGOTH and an IQ test use numbers. Six red lights mean more lying than two red lights. A score of 136 means more intelligence than a score of 102. If you can count, it is all quite clear. HAGOTH and an IQ test provide us with what are called "objective answers." Thus, we achieve precision.

Third, both HAGOTH and an IQ test are simple. Philosophers may sweat the question "What is truth?" in books that are a burden to carry, let alone read. HAGOTH bypasses all of this complexity and doubt. If you have a telephone, you have immediate access to the answer. Similarly, intelligence may be elusive to those who must rely on observing how people cope with their problems, and such judgments require time and multivarious situations. The answer comes both fast and easily through an IQ test.

What we are dealing with here is one of the more overbearing and, of course, dangerous teachings of our information environment. As such, it is necessary for educators to recognize it and, as I want to argue, to oppose it vigorously. I am referring to the idea that it is only through the use of *technique* and *technicalization* that we may find out what is real, what is true, and what is valuable. In its extreme form, this idea amounts to a religious conception, which I have elsewhere called "Eichmannism": the belief that technique is the Supreme Authority and the measure of all things. Both HAGOTH and an IQ test are products of this belief. They do more than merely give us information. They put forward an argument which I will call here the Technical Thesis. In this chapter I want to reveal that argument, and to suggest that there are alternative arguments that we must not keep concealed from our children. The issue, like the one dealt with in the last two chapters, is about the biases of our information environment. What is at stake is how our children will manage their intellect.

Before proceeding, however, I must make it clear that I raise no objections against the rational use of technique to achieve human purposes. We are technical creatures, and it is in our predilection for and our ability to create techniques that we achieve high levels of clarity and efficiency. Language itself is technique, and through it we achieve more than clarity and efficiency. We achieve humanity. Or inhumanity. For the question with language, as with other techniques, is and always has been, Who is to be the master? Will we control it, or will it control us? Thus, my argument is not against technique, without which we would be less than human; my argument is with the triumph of technique, which means technique that subordinates and even obliterates human purpose, technique that directs us to serve *its* purposes, not our own.

What, then, are technique and its progeny, technicalization? This is a complicated matter, which I will here try to simplify by saying that technique is a standardized method for achieving a purpose. It may be embodied in machinery or language or numbers or any sort of material that can be made to repeat itself, including, of course, human behavior. In fact, human behavior is itself the fundamental paradigm of technique, for at every level—from physiological to social —we reproduce our behaviors. We are, in a sense, our own clones. Our talk, our dress, our manners, our movements— these are all repetitions of previous behaviors, executed to insure predictability and control, and governed by a set of rules. The rules may not always be known to us, as is the case with those that direct our physiological processes. But they are there nonetheless. Without them our blood would not circulate through our bodies, our cells would not regenerate themselves. It is the same with language, for the sentences we produce are not randomly formed. They are governed by rules of formation and transformation which we have only recently become aware of and do not yet fully grasp. And it is the same with our social behavior, although here we know quite a bit about the nature of the rules since we have consciously established them to serve specific purposes. For example, a classroom is an ensemble of techniques for standardizing and controlling behavior. So are a courtroom, a restaurant, and a highway. We can write down the rules that govern these situations, and even teach them in a systematic way.[2]

Our artifacts, and in particular our machinery, also are governed by rules, and are designed not only to standardize *our* behavior but to standardize their own. An airplane so constructed that it obeys the laws of physics only occasionally is useless, as is a thermometer that responds to heat only when it is "in the mood." We say of such machines that they are "broken," by which we mean their behavior is random, unstandardized, unreliable.

Thus, as I have said, we are technical creatures, and our standardized behavior and machinery—our techniques—

make up most of what we call our culture. In saying this, I am saying nothing that is not obvious to everyone. But it sometimes happens that technique begins to function independently of the system it serves. It becomes autonomous, in the manner of a robot that no longer obeys its master. The "purposes" of technique somehow come to dominate a situation, and thereby become a danger to it. The robot, of course, always attacks its master first. Cancer, for example, is a "normal" physiological technique over which we have lost control. Cells regenerate themselves according to blind genetic instructions, without any coordination with the rest of the organism. The body then exists to serve the "purposes" of the process, not the other way around. In a similar way, neurosis is a linguistic technique that has become more important than our own effectiveness. When we generate sentences that produce unsatisfactory results for us, yet cannot stop doing so, then we are in the service of our sentences, not in the service of ourselves.

There are many names for this aberrant process by which a method for doing something becomes the reason for doing it. At the cultural level, one of the names is *reification.* To reify a procedure or a technique is to elevate it to the status of a purposeful creature, to invest it with objectives of its own. To reify is more than to put the cart before the horse, which is merely bad technique. It is to make sure that both the cart and the horse get where they are going, even if the passenger does not. It is to forget that neither a cart nor a horse has any place to go, that they are the means to a human purpose.

But in order for reification of technique to occur certain conditions must obtain, and the most important of these is what may be called *technicalization.* Technicalization is itself a technique. It is a method of transforming a technique into an abstract, general, and precise system. To build a boat requires technique. To draw plans and a set of instructions for building a boat is technicalization. To assess the truth of another's remarks requires technique. To construct HAGOTH is technicalization. To judge someone's intelligence requires technique. To construct an IQ test is technicalization. In other words, technicalization objectifies technique. It removes technique from a specific context, separates the doer from the doing, and therefore eliminates individuality. Whereas technique is a standardized method for doing something, technicalization standardizes the standard. To technicalize is to reduce all possible techniques to one method, to convert *a* method into *the* method. Technicalization enshrines technique and renders it invariant. It is technique writ large and inviolate.[3]

All cultures are products of technique. Only some are products of technicalization. Through technicalization we can achieve prodigious scientific and industrial feats, but there is a price to pay. Paradoxically, by objectifying and sanctifying technique, we hide from ourselves what techniques are for. In a culture burdened by technicalization, we must spend most of our time learning the proper methods: learning how to read the plans, learning how to correlate the numbers, learning how to adjust the dials. There is little time to reflect on their purpose or to consider alternative methods. As a consequence, our commitment is to the integrity of our techniques, to the development of our expertise, and to the preservation of our technical definitions and directions. And therein lies the problem. We come to reify our procedures: to believe that procedure supercedes purpose, that in fact procedure is more real than purpose. For to reject a procedure is to challenge the basis on which a technicalized culture rests. Such a culture can survive purposes not achieved. What it cannot survive are procedures that are ignored.

It hardly needs to be said that one of the powerful devices for achieving technicalization is the use of numbers, against which mortals always seem to be defenseless. Imagine someone shouting to you on the telephone, "Help me, please! There's a fire here, my leg's broken, and I can't move. Help! Please!" Your HAGOTH would register considerable stress in the person's voice. All eight red lights would flash. Hence, the caller is deceiving you. By numerical definition. Numbers give precision to definitions, and in a technicalized culture it is precision we want. If the caller is really in danger, so much the worse for him. The machine works. And so it does, in a sense, for in a technicalized culture, what the machine measures becomes, ultimately, the reality.

Everyone must have a favorite and real example of the tyranny of numbers. Mine is a scene from high-school days. Because I had received an eighty-three in English, I missed by a fraction being eligible for Arista. I approached my English teacher, a gentle and sensitive man, as I remember, and requested that he reassess my performance with a view toward elevating my grade two points. He regarded my request as reasonable and studiously examined his record book. Then he turned toward me, with genuine sadness in his face, and said, "I'm sorry, Neil. You're an eighty-three. An eighty-four at most, but not an eighty-five. Not this term, anyway."

The point is that we were both crazy, my English teacher and I. He, because he believed I was an eighty-three or eighty-four at most, and I, because I believed his belief. He had been fair. He had reviewed the numbers, which were both precise and objective. To him, my performance *was* the numbers. To me, as well. This is reification of technique, from which, several years later, I began to recover almost completely. I often wonder if he got better, too. The disease is not, however, so easy to overcome, because ultimately technicalization is more than a bias of culture. It is a bias of mind. Its assumptions become an interior voice which excludes alternative modes of perception.

What does it take for a teacher to believe, really believe,

that a student *is* an eighty-three (or eighty-four at most)? It requires, first of all, a belief that it is possible to reduce a person or his behavior to numbers. It requires a total acceptance of the symbols and definitions of a technical system. It requires a belief that a system which supplies precision is, by that virtue, objective and hence, real. It requires, above all, a belief that the technical system can do your thinking for you—that is to say, it requires that calculation supersede judgment.

I remember another instance in my school career that, in a metaphorical way, will help me to show the power and range of the technical thesis. This time the scene was a college classroom, where I was taking a course in health. The professor was giving a lecture on the incidence of hunger throughout the world. She concluded with the remark that it can be well documented that at least six billion children go to sleep hungry each night. Our class did not know much about these things, but we knew that there were certainly not more than three billion people on Earth—which would make her statement a logical impossibility. The point was raised. She looked startled for a moment. Checked her notes. Then said, somewhat relieved, "I know it doesn't sound right, but that's what I've got here."

Now, at first thought, one might say what we have here is just a stupid professor, or one who has merely made a mistake and is too embarrassed to acknowledge it. But there is more to it than this. Even if she were aware that her remark was preposterous, it is significant that she believed it was an acceptable excuse to refer us to the fact that the remark was suitably enshrined in her notes. Her notes were, so to speak, a closed and self-confirming system. Her defense was the equivalent of saying that eight green lights have flashed, hence, her statement is true.

This sort of thinking is quite common in our schools, and in fact it is so well established that special names have been invented to cover "mistakes," which, by the way, are not acknowledged as mistakes. I refer, for example, to the words "overachiever" and "underachiever." What is an "over-achiever"? It is someone whose score on a standardized IQ test is relatively low—say, a ninety-four—but whose real-life intellectual performance is consistently high. In other words, the test can't be wrong. The student *is* a ninety-four. He merely insists on behaving as if he were not. Perhaps there is even something perverse in him. Certainly, there is an element of perversity in the underachiever—someone whose test score is relatively high but who does not perform well in other respects. The point is that the test score is taken as the reality. The student's behavior in various contexts is to be judged against this standard. If life contradicts a test score, so much the worse for life. Life makes mistakes. Instruments do not.

Schools, however, are not by any means the most dedicated promoters of the Technical Thesis. One may find the thesis advanced in almost every social institution, in a variety of ways and with varying degrees of ardor. The technical thesis consists of more than the tendency to reduce people to numerical abstractions. Its essence is to get people to submit themselves to the sovereignty of exclusive definitions and formal procedures. In this sense, there is no more powerful expression of the technical thesis than in the development of the state itself. The modern state is pure technicalization, consisting of little else but definitions, procedures, and the means of commanding obedience to them. One of the astonishing political ironies of our own time is the homage paid to large-scale technicalization by "liberals" and "humanists" who in wishing to expand human freedom have turned consistently to the formal structure of government for assistance. The guiding principle here would seem to be: That government is best which governs most completely, and most precisely.

It is not enough, apparently, that government should protect against minority discrimination. Government must also insure minority equality. It is not enough that government should care for people who are ill. Government must insure that they are healthy. It is not even enough that government should protect children against child abuse. It must also protect parents against "child responsibility" (for it is sometimes inconvenient for parents to tend their own children, in which case government should be available to provide a remedy).

I do not wish to argue here that any particular responsibility given to government is either good or bad. That is the subject of another book by a different author. Rather, I wish to point to the political dangers of the technical thesis, which reside in this invariant rule: When technical organizations (that is, bureaucracies) are given power to do something, they always take more of it than is actually needed. Tests, computers, machines, *and* governments share this propensity. They always end up controlling more ground than one imagines had been given to them. Thus, in yielding to government the sovereignty to implement a "humane" purpose, we always sacrifice some dimension of freedom we had not intended to give. This is the technical trap to which Jacques Ellul refers in his phrase "the political illusion," the idea that every conceivable problem of social relations may be solved by submitting it to the domain of technical control, i.e., a political solution. The precise cost is that we immerse ourselves in techniques far beyond our capacity to master them. That we have been so eager to do this is a tribute to the power of the technical thesis and its fundamental presupposition: Only through objective, formal, and precise standardization can we control our lives. In other words, through machinery.

This thesis carries far beyond our political and social life. It ultimately forms the core of a religious conception. I have, for example, previously made reference to the "religious" nature of television programs by pointing to their parabolic content. In considering what are the messages of these parables, we may see how deeply the technical thesis cuts, how it comes to form a modern equivalent of the Sermon on the Mount. TV commercials, especially, show this with astonishing clarity. What is the solution to each problem posed by a TV commercial? Where are we directed to seek, and what are we told we will find? The answer is that we shall find peace and happiness through the ministrations of technology. It may be animal technology, vegetable technology, or mineral technology but it is always technology. That is what we must commune with, that is what we must strive toward. The commercials tell us that, somewhere, there is a drug, a detergent, or a machine to deliver us from whatever shocks our flesh is heir to. Boredom, anxiety, fear, envy, sloth— there are remedies for each of these, and more. The remedies are called Scope, Comet, Cordova, Whisper Jet, Bufferin, and Pabst. They take the place of good works, piety, awe, humility, and transcendence.

On TV commercials, in other words, there do not really exist moral deficiencies as we customarily think of them. Nor are there intimations of the conventional roads to spiritual redemption. But there *is* Original Sin, and it consists in our having been ignorant of a technique or a technology which offers happiness. We may achieve a state of grace by attending to the good news about it, which will appear every six or seven minutes. It follows from this that that person is most devout who knows of the largest array of technologies, and he is a heretic who willfully ignores what is there to be used.

It is, of course, also part of this religion that people must think of themselves as little more than machines. Like machines, we must submit ourselves to continuous improvement. In fact, it is alleged that we exhibit a certain measure of moral weakness in resisting the opportunities to become new models. Do you think your hair is nice? It isn't. It can be made brighter and softer. Do you think you are attractive? You aren't. You can make yourself thinner or healthier. Do you think you are efficient? You are not. You can improve your productivity threefold. What's more, you are under a moral compulsion of sorts to do so. Would the Ford Motor Company sell, in 1980, a 1979 model? How can you do the same with yourself? Like machinery, you must progress, streamline, and polish yourself, present yourself as forever new.

All of this—technology as salvation—is what Christine Nystrom calls the "metaphysics" of the content of television, by which she means its principal assumptions about what is at the core of human failings and about how we may overcome them.[4] This is another way of saying that television presents us with the technical thesis as a religious conception, an ultimate concern around which people organize their motivations and actions. And we find it preached not only in commercials but on what are called "programs." On action television, typically, the resolution of the struggle between good guys and bad does not recommend to us the force of a traditional moral imperative. It recommends to us the efficacy of a superior technology, technique, or technical organization. Kojak, Starsky, Hutch, Rockford, Jones, et al., are not in any clearcut terms very much morally superior to their adversaries. Not in a traditional sense, they aren't. However, according to the Technical Religion, they *are* morally superior in that their technical skills prevail. Their cars are better, their guns are better, their aim is better, their procedures are better, their organization is better.

What needs to be noticed is that the masters of the media have quite simply preempted the functions of religious leaders in articulating the moral values by which we ought to live. From this point of view, the excessive violence on TV, to which so many object, is not nearly so important an issue as is TV's replacement of the traditional moral code with the

Technical Thesis. Even where action shows have reduced significantly their displays of violence, they still stand as celebrations of technique. *Mission: Impossible,* which had relatively few instances of overt violence, was a weekly parable on the virtue, indeed the glory, of technicalization. Its heroes were not people but techniques. Its bad guys were people whose most glaring weakness was their failure to know about or sufficiently appreciate the efficacy of sophisticated machinery. In this sense, *Mission: Impossible* was the most religious program on the TV schedule. And we can be sure that its teachings were not ignored.

In the more benign TV programs such as "family shows," we find no violence, but nonetheless the technical thesis is there in full force. Almost without exception, the problems which are the focus of each program are about breakdowns or misunderstandings in human relations. There rarely arise moral questions of a traditional sort. There are only questions of how to manage one's human relations. This is surely not an insignificant matter but the point is that living is construed as purely a technical problem. One may solve the problem through amiability or increased communication or artful concealment. But the message of the parable is clear enough: The central human concern is not one's relationship to moral imperatives but one's technique in solving the problems of relationship-management. To put it simply, God is not dead. He survives as Technique.

It is important to say here that I am not contending that TV or other electronic media have created the technical thesis. That they amplify, explicate, and celebrate it is beyond doubt. But its origins are to be found elsewhere. Lewis Mumford believes that the age of the "mega-machine," i.e., large-scale technicalization, began with the building of the pyramids, the first instance of the massive and systematic use of people as machines. Harold Innis suggests that technicalization began with the printing press, the first example of mass production of communications. Jacques Ellul implies that the invention of the mechanical clock was the first example of the widespread subjugation of human organization to the sovereignty of a machine, from which, he believes, we have never recovered. Ortega y Gasset argues that industrialization which produced the specialist and "mass man" also produced a sort of mindless technical man. And Chaim Perelman links the origin of the technical thesis to an age-old desire to be, like God, perfect, such perfection being attainable through precision and objectivity.

It is not to my purpose to settle this question, even if I had the wit and learning to do it. The fact is that in our own time, the technical thesis is advanced so vigorously and on so many fronts that it has created an ecological problem, and a dangerous one. We have a generation being raised in an information environment that, on one hand, stresses visual imagery, discontinuity, immediacy, and alogicality. It is antihistorical, antiscientific, anticonceptual, antirational. On the other hand, the context within which this occurs is a kind of religious or philosophic bias toward the supreme authority of technicalization. What this means is that as we lose confidence and competence in our ability to think and judge, we willingly transfer these functions to machines. Whereas our machinery was once thought of as an "extension of man," man now becomes an "extension of machinery." It is no accident that so much energy is being devoted to the development, in computer technology, of "artificial intelligence," the purpose of which is to eliminate human judgment altogether. Or, if not that, to create a situation in which only a few people who are in control of the machinery have the authority to exercise human judgment. He who controls the definitions and rules of technique becomes the master, especially in a situation where people lack the intellectual ability and motivation to understand the assumptions of the technical thesis.

In saying all of this, I am not preparing an argument for a Luddite response, as, for example, the thesis one finds in *Four Arguments for the Elimination of Television*. We gain nothing but chaos by banning or breaking our machines or indiscriminately disassembling our social machinery. Although at some time in the future such measures could be taken, they would be the ultimate acts of hysteria of people who live by techniques and who lack the intellectual resources to domesticate them. As Ortega y Gasset remarks, when the masses, in despair and revolt, go searching for bread, their tendency is to destroy the bakeries. In the end, technique is not our enemy. We are. Where then do we turn to protect ourselves against ourselves?

The answers to this question have been given many times and with great eloquence by such people as Lewis Mumford, Jacques Ellul, Erich Fromm, Norbert Wiener, Arthur Koestler, Joseph Weizenbaum, Karl Popper, Marshall McLuhan, and Jacob Bronowski. They all tell us, first and foremost, that we may find protection in the development of our intellect and judgment, and in our continuing quest for knowledge of ourselves and our artifacts. Some of them tell us that we may find protection in the power of those traditional values which stress personal autonomy, community cohesion, family loyalty, and the primacy of human affection. And some also tell us that without a traditional basis of moral authority, we are totally disarmed. We are warned that expertise is no substitute for piety and awe, that efficiency is no substitute for sensitivity and affection, that the state is no substitute for the family, that bureaucracy is no substitute for civilized social relations, that machinery is no substitute for a sense of transcendence.

All of these answers and warnings seem to me unassailable although it is far from clear how in our present information environment any movement can be made toward acting on them. But certainly this is precisely where the schools can help us. We must not, of course, make the mistake of believing that schools may, in any sense, be our salvation, and in the next chapter I want to discuss the question of the limitations of schooling. But one thing is clear: If the schools themselves can avoid falling victim to the Technical Thesis they may serve as a useful antidote to it, and thereby assist in giving balance to the education of our young. This is an enormous "if," since the schools have already shown themselves to be easily accessible to the biases of the Technical Thesis.

Consider, for example, the extent to which schools have welcomed the encroachment of standardized tests of every conceivable variety, "objective measurement," and such vulgarities as "competency-based performance." Moreover, that at any time or place, schools would use what are called "IQ tests" is enough to make one despair of the hope that we may use the schools as a corrective to the technical thesis. As far as I am concerned, the following quotation by Joseph Weizenbaum of MIT says very nearly all that needs to be said on the subject of IQ testing, or the HAGOTH mentality:

> Few "scientific" concepts have so thoroughly muddled the thinking of both scientists and the general public as that of the "intelligence quotient" or "IQ." The idea that intelligence can be quantitatively measured along a simple linear scale has caused untold harm to our society in general, and to education in particular. It has spawned, for example, the huge educational-testing movement in the United States, which strongly influences the courses of the academic careers of millions of students and thus the degrees of certification they may attain. It virtually determines what "success" people may achieve in later life because, in the United States at least, opportunities to "succeed" are, by and large, open only to those who have the proper credentials, that is, university degrees, professional diplomas, and so on.[5]

Or, as David McClelland has said, "Psychologists should be ashamed of themselves for promoting a view of general intelligence that has engendered such a testing program." But if psychologists should be ashamed of themselves, then educators should go further by donning hair shirts and scourging themselves with nettles. And yet the outside pressures on the schools to continue to technicalize their operation are continuous, the most burdensome recent example being the "back to the basics" movement. As far as I understand it, this movement for education reform has its origins in a genuinely felt dissatisfaction with the ability of the young to cope with digital symbolism, i.e., reading, writing, and arithmetic. The response to the problem is to place instruction, learning, and evaluation under the jurisdiction of a precise technical system so that at any point what is happening can be described in quantifiable terms. Moreover, any subject whose absorption does not lend itself to quantifiable description is, by definition, not regarded as basic. This is, of course, the response of the technocrat, of people who believe that HAGOTH is more to be trusted than human judgment. For such people the very language of education must be converted into HAGOTHian terms. We are required to talk of "input" and "output," of "quality control," of "behavioral objectives," all of which have been taken directly from the world of industrialization, not of learning.

In such a vocabulary, students are objects or commodities, mere units in some statistical compilation. In the usual "back to the basics" formulation of our problem, the solution lies in improving our statistics, not our students. Students are to learn what will show up as a number. If something that is learned cannot be precisely measured, it does not exist.

Of course, a statistic requires a large sample to give it force —the larger the better. Statistics, in this way, become an instrument for political control, requiring more and more students to be subjected to their sovereignty. And since the technocrat-reformers, backed by the power of the technical thesis, have persuaded so many people that precision and objectivity are to be sought above all else, so much greater will be the tendency to standardize instruction and evaluation. Thus, the ideal situation is for everyone to be taught the same thing at the same time by the same methods, and judged by the same measures. Then we will know who is an eighty-three and who is not. We will know if our schools are "improving," and if our students are getting "better."

There are two essential points to be made about this bias. The first is that it redefines what we mean by education and learning, and that its definitions are wholly controlled by what instruments are available to quantify learning; that is to say, it is reductionist and impoverishing. The second point is the less obvious observation that such a bias is an entirely revolutionary idea. We are accustomed to thinking of "radicals" as young, disaffected people, far from the mainstream of the institutions they wish to overturn. We think of them as wearing unconventional attire and using fierce and shocking language. We do not usually think of a revolutionary as a person wearing a three-piece suit, commanding a comfortable salary and job security. Yet, in this instance, that is exactly what we have, for I think it can justly be said that the Educational Testing Service in Princeton, New Jersey, is one of the most revolutionary institutions in the United States. It is the supreme seat of technicalization of education in the country. Its managers and its customers are, for the most part, stable, comfortable, and successful people. For all that, they make the Weathermen look like archconservatives. Their rhetoric is neither fierce nor shocking, to be sure. It is the reasonable rhetoric of the technical thesis: Let us measure everything for everyone. Let us produce objective information. We will conquer subjectivity. We will eliminate complexity and ambiguity, and replace them with precision. In this way we will always know how we are doing.

But in this way one never gets to consider the question of what we are doing, or ought to be doing. Or whether or not it is, in any sense, desirable to place education in the domain of statistics, for the instruments settle all questions of purpose in advance. Technique becomes an education philosophy, just as it becomes a political ideology or a religious code. It determines what shall be done in school, and how, and how much. It is this philosophy that I regard as both revolutionary and dangerous. In no sense does it represent a going back to anything. The reduction of education to the simplistic mechanisms of objective testing represents a turning away from the profound questions we expect an education philosophy to address. It is a rejection of the past, for there have been no people anywhere who have done or have even contemplated doing what is proposed by our vast educational-testing bureaucracies. Moreover, by allowing the bias of technicalization to preempt all other philosophies, we place our schools in the service of the very ideology that requires the severest criticism.

The situation is hardly encouraging. And yet, the schools represent the best card we can play. They have a tradition of humane concern and a conservative bias. There is among many teachers a suspicion of technicalization and a keen awareness of its limitations. There is even among parents a certain resistance to submitting their children to the autonomy of technique. It is far from fanciful that the schools can generate a counterargument to the technical thesis, an argument that denies the intrinsic authority of technical definitions, that speaks in favor of ambiguity and complexity, that refuses to accept efficiency as a definitive purpose or technique as a comprehensive philosophy. The well-heeled revolutionaries will do anything to prevent such arguments from entering the schools, which is why they adore the "back to the basics" movement. The schools nonetheless offer a hopeful possibility, provided they are not rendered impotent by the Utopian Thesis, to which we must now turn.

6

The Utopian Thesis

The late Wendell Johnson developed an idea which he encapsulated in the phrase "the IFD disease." I have written about this idea in three books, but in none of them has it more applicability than in this one. Thus, I will repeat myself, with, I believe, good cause.

The letters *I, F,* and *D* are the initials of the words *Idealization, Frustration,* and *Demoralization.* As Johnson used the term, the IFD disease denotes a psychological progression, or more accurately, a regression, from a state of relative optimism and apparent clarity to a state of despair and confusion. The way it works is this: A person tries to establish for himself or herself a goal or a set of goals. As is natural and inevitable, the goal must be expressed in language—specifically, in an internalized sentence. The sentence might be something like "I want to be rich," or "I want to be happy," or "I want to be successful." Such sentences can be extremely dangerous, because many people who use them do not have a clear idea of what they mean by the words "rich," "happy," and "successful." In fact, some people have no idea whatsoever. Therefore, under the inspiration of a sentence such as "I want to be successful," a person may start on a journey for which there is no destination. In such a case, the word "successful" has been idealized. It is a name for which there is no correlate in objective reality. It is, in short, the equivalent of a nonsense word, as if one were to say, "I want to be ratchety." If you do not know the referent for ratchety (or successful), you cannot know if you have ever achieved it, or even *how* to.

Of course, any word can be made to assume an intelligible and achievable meaning. You can say that rich means making thirty thousand dollars a year. Or that successful means giving birth to a healthy baby. Or that happy means being able to start your car in the morning when it is nine degrees below zero. But there are many people who do not take themselves through this stage—that is, of operationalizing their meanings. Thus, armed with maps for which there are no territories, they become frustrated at their failure to achieve ratchetiness, and eventually they become demoralized altogether.[1]

The IFD disease, in other words, is a diagnosis of the emotional difficulties of certain individuals. And it is commonplace for counselors and psychotherapists to use the solution which the diagnosis suggests. That solution is to have people review very carefully what sorts of sentences they have been using as life goals—whether long-term or short—and to have them exorcise those words which cannot lead to realistic and satisfying results.

For reasons which I am unable to discern, the idea of the IFD disease has not been widely applied to the analysis of social and political difficulties. This is puzzling because it seems obvious to me that it may account for some of the recurring problems within our social institutions. This is certainly true of our educational system. At almost no time in its long history have many people been satisfied with it. It is a source of continual frustration and even demoralization.

And although many people have made creative proposals to fix it, nothing seems to help. Why? I should like to suggest that one reason is the IFD disease or, as I should like to call it here, the Utopian Thesis.

Almost the last person to phrase educational goals in realistic and achievable terms was Thomas Jefferson. He believed the goal of schooling should be to help people protect themselves against tyranny. He operationalized this goal by specifying a curriculum which included the study of reading, writing, mathematics, and history. He believed that the study of these subjects would provide people with sufficient competence in critical, logical, and historical thinking so that they would have the will and ability to understand and argue their own causes and to understand and resist causes hostile to their own liberty. That schools should also assume the responsibility of providing youth with motivation to learn or emotional stability or sex education would probably have struck Jefferson as ridiculous on the face of it—and for two reasons: first, because he would doubt the ability of the schools to accomplish such goals, and second, because he would regard such matters as none of the schools' business.

But Jeffersonian restraint, modesty, and realism have not prevailed in our educational history. As Henry Perkinson has documented in his book *The Imperfect Panacea,* Americans have not hesitated to use their public schools as instruments to solve the myriad and intractable social and political problems their other institutions have been unable to handle. Historically the schools have taken on such goals as de-ethnicizing the immigrant population, preparing youth for entry into the job market, and training children to become avid consumers and bank-using, insurance-minded, money-saving citizens. Within our own lifetime, we have seen the schools go into the sex-education business, the drug-education business, the driver-education business, the brotherhood business, the psychological counseling business, the free-lunch business, the baby-sitting business, the racial integration business, the social equality business, the motivation business, and lately, the business of *ethnicizing* the population, after having failed in de-ethnicizing it.

The problem with all of these goals is twofold. First, in classic IFD terms, some of them have been phrased in such vague and nonoperational terms that they were and are doomed to failure. The schools, for example, do not have a very clear idea of what they mean by motivation or sex education or even ethnicizing the population. But just as important, even where the schools can operationalize their goals—as with driver education or drug education—we find that the goal agenda of the schools is so full, so complicated, even so contradictory that almost nothing of enduring value can be accomplished. It is as if so many goals are written on the wall that the wall falls down. As a consequence, teachers, administrators, and parents, not to mention the children, are continuously frustrated by the inadequate results of the schooling process, and some of them eventually become demoralized. This is inevitably the outcome of utopianism.

I wish to emphasize here that I do not regard the schools' goal agenda as being overloaded with frills. Of all the charges made by "back to the basics" advocates, that is the silliest. There is nothing "frilly" about brotherhood, ethnic pride, motivation, sex education, or psychological counseling. The problem is just the opposite. The schools have assumed the burden of solving extremely important problems, but they are simply not equipped to achieve the solutions. If you heap upon the school all of the problems that the family, the church, the political system, and the economy cannot solve, the school becomes a kind of well-financed garbage dump, from which very little can be expected except the unsweet odor of failure.

As I have previously said, the idea of mass public education is an American invention, one of the original and important contributions we have so far made to world civilization. But having conceived of it, we have proceeded to undermine its fulfillment by afflicting it with impossible dreams. The route to relief is, of course, to review the ways in which we have stated our educational goals, the number and variety of those goals, and the realism of those goals. And then to rid ourselves of those which cannot lead us toward authentic achievement.

In this context the "back to the basics" movement has made a useful contribution in that it reproaches educators for their ambitions and expansionism. One might even say that, in this reproach, "back to the basics" represents sound conservative doctrine, advancing as it does two important and interrelated criticisms. The first is that schools are technical organizations, and like all such bureaucracies will tend to exemplify the technical thesis: They will try to control more and more of people's lives. The school, after all, is an agency of the state. And although conservatives are not always consistent on this point, in general they are wary of the state's encroachment on the personal liberties of individuals. The second criticism is that the schools have accepted without much forethought what C. P. Snow calls "the liberal package," the principal ingredients of which are the assumptions that all problems are environmental in their origin and that individuals cannot, therefore, be held accountable for their failings. The liberal faith holds that expanding and vigorous social engineering will solve whatever problems arise, and that the schools are one of the chief instrumentalities for this effort. So, what we have witnessed in schools is not only a widening of their scope, but a shifting of the focus of responsibility from individuals in particular to society in general.

Although liberals are not always consistent on this point either, their position has tended to be that people are not in control of their own lives, that they are most accurately viewed as "victims" of institutional failure, and that not only poverty but everything from stupidity to irresponsibility are social diseases rather than individual failings. Since the liberal faith has had wide acceptance, this has meant that schools have inevitably gone into the business of reforming society, not individuals, and accounts for the increasing number of utopian items on the schools' agenda. I am not unaware that my own agenda for the schools is based on certain social problems that have arisen and that have "victimized" individuals. I am therefore in no position to reject categorically the "liberal" assumptions. But the conservative view nonetheless forces us to pay attention to the limits of social engineering and to the dangers of utopianism. In its most thoughtful expression, the "back to the basics" movement raises the questions, How much can a school do? To what extent shall we permit schools to take over the functions of other institutions, such as the family and the church? In what respects is it self-defeating to blame society and not individuals for certain problems? To what extent are liberal reformers merely technocrats, operating under the sway of the technical thesis?

These are, in my view, extremely useful questions. And it is a pity that so many of the "back to the basics" advocates are themselves crass technocrats who would reduce the schools' objectives to the most simplistic, mechanistic, and trivial goals. They often deny communities the opportunity to engage in a serious and creative argument about what is both worth doing in schools and what really can be done by the schools. The outcome of such an argument would be the development of some limiting principles which on the one hand would permit schools to pursue objectives of high aspiration and profound meaning, but on the other would keep their programs within modest and restrained perimeters.

In the preceding pages I have tried to offer two such limiting principles. The first, of course, is the principle with which the book begins: The schools should always provide an alternative educational bias to the educational bias of the rest of the culture. This is the countercyclical or thermostatic view of schools and, as I have tried to explain, is justified by the principles of social ecology. Without opposition, the biases of a culture turn in on themselves, overrun the culture, and become dangerously oppressive. But it is obvious that schools cannot offer alternatives to every bias of the culture. If they were to attempt it, their agenda would be even more crowded and confused than it presently is, and the consequent failures of the schools would be even more pronounced than they are. That is why, in Chapters Two through Five, I have in effect added another limiting principle: The schools should focus their attention on the information environment and, in particular, on the *structure* of the information environment. This means that educators would be centrally concerned with the topology of information—its form, its speed, its magnitude, its direction, its accessibility, its continuity— and ultimately, with the bias of mind that any information configuration would tend to promote. It is obvious that values are by no means outside the scope of such a concern. For example, the antiscientific, antihistorical, and immediacy biases of electronic information are as much a matter of values as they are a matter of intellect. What I have called the technical thesis is in fact almost wholly a set of values promoted by the character of our particular information environment. By offering the idea that it is the business of schools to provide a countervailing education to the biases of the structure of information within the culture, I am not proposing to reduce the educator to the status of a teacher of skills.

From a conservative point of view, the teacher, to be sure, would be teaching those skills that contemporary culture suppresses, but such teachings would of necessity include attitudes and habits of mind that our revolutionary information environment mocks and even despises, but without which a person cannot be fully educated. In the remaining chapters of this book, I want to indicate explicitly and precisely what skills and attitudes these are, and how they might be communicated. Here, I want to add one more limiting and conservative principle which seems to me essential to observe if schools are to strengthen themselves, our youth, and our society. I refer to the idea that schools should not, except under the most extreme provocation, try to accomplish goals which other social institutions traditionally serve. This principle is implied by the previous two—namely, that the schools should act as a thermostat and that they should do so by offering alternatives to our prevailing information environment. In other words, there is no other institution in our society that is designed to perform these tasks or that has any motivation to perform them. Neither is there any institution so well prepared to take them on. But there are institutions such as the family, the church, the medical profession, and community and political organizations that have quite specific functions which the schools ought not to intrude upon, though they have continuously done so.

There are three reasons why schools should avoid such intrusions. The first is that teachers are not competent to serve as priests, psychologists, therapists, political reformers, social workers, sex advisors, or parents. That they wish to do so is understandable, since in this way they may elevate their prestige. That they would feel it necessary to do so is also understandable, since so many social institutions, including the family and the church, have deteriorated in their structure and meaning, leaving children bereft of the support that these institutions might be expected to give them. But incompetent teachers are not an improvement on ineffective social institutions, and all the prattle in the world about teaching "the whole child" does not change the fact that there is nothing in the background or education of teachers that prepares them to do what other institutions are supposed to do. I hope it is clear that by incompetent teachers I do not mean that teachers cannot do *their* work. I mean that teachers cannot do *everyone's* work. Among several ill-advised remarks made by America's greatest education philosopher, John Dewey, perhaps the most misguided is his statement that "the teacher . . . always is the true prophet of God and the usherer in of the true Kingdom of God." It is to be doubted that Dewey consulted with God on this matter. Or vice versa. While it is true that God's prophets may come from the most humble origins and unexpected places, nowhere, except in Dewey's grandiose vision, can I find authority for this assignment. It is more seemly to suppose that ushering in the Kingdom of God is work to be shared among many groups, each with its special competence to assist and improve people. The belief that this mission should be undertaken mainly by teachers is, to use Dewey's metaphor, likely to lead us directly into Satan's dwelling. And this for another reason, aside from the unpreparedness and limitations of teachers: The more one social institution encroaches upon the functions of another, the more it weakens it. This idea, incidentally, also comes from the field of ecology, where it is understood that as one system begins to preempt the purposes of another, the functional capacity of both is undermined. If the school, for example, assumes the prerogatives normally exercised by the family, the family loses some of its motivation, authority, and competence to provide what it is designed to do. We have already seen this principle operate in relation to psychiatry and religion. Some years ago Karl Menninger asked, in the title of one of his books, Whatever became of sin? The answer is that psychology has redefined it, called it guilt (of all things, an erroneous zone!), has tried to show how debilitating it is and how one may get rid of it through psychological strategies. All of this has been done in the name of science, and possibly, one might add, in the interests of commerce, since it costs more money to exorcise guilt in a psychiatrist's office than to redeem oneself from sin in a church. But sin is not to be dispensed with so easily; we have it still, but we also have less faith in the capacity of our religious institutions to help us understand and cope with it. In fact, since our clerics now behave like psychologists and our psychologists like clerics, it is hard to know, sometimes, if one has entered a church or a psychiatric clinic. In any event, the psychiatrists cannot eliminate sin, and the clerics, as Menninger wrote, have lost confidence in the power of their own discipline to deal with it. This is an example of the pollution of social environments, the mixing of modes of discourse and areas of competence. It results in confusion rather than clarity.

As between the family and school, we have a similar confusion. Where, for example, did the radical idea come from that the school is largely responsible for motivating children to learn? Or that it should instruct them in the moral dimensions of sex? Or that it should teach children to save money? These teachings, it seems to me, are the prerogatives and responsibilities of families, not state agencies, and the fact that some families do not exercise these prerogatives and responsibilities well is no justification for the school to assume the right to do so. In the following pages, I wish to identify, merely as examples, a few areas into which schools have intruded, and to make some brief comments on why these incursions are a mistake. But the principal point to be made here is that as the school blurs the lines of authority between itself and other institutions, it tends to weaken not only its own capabilities but the capabilities of the other institutions as well. We have already reached a point where people are quite willing to place their children in schools (called, I believe, Day Care centers) at age two, and expect such schools to socialize them, provide them with emotional security, and teach them moral values, discipline, intellectual skills, creativity, good eating and elimination habits, a healthy attitude toward sex, and tolerance for all people. Aside from the fact that no school can effectively do all this, what is left for the children's parents to do? Perhaps only to decide which school to send their children to. The state takes it from there. It would appear that many parents do not care to have a "family life," or to accept the traditional responsibilities of parent-teachers. Perhaps many have even been made to feel by the schools' ready assumption of their prerogatives that they are incapable of parenting, that the school knows how to do all these things and that they do not. In any event, the diminished scope of family responsibility is an extremely serious problem for all of us, and the school must decline to participate in its further erosion. The family is unquestionably the most important buffer between the individual and the state. It is, for example, one of the few remaining informal—i.e., nontechnicalized—institutions which have a serious claim on the loyalties of individuals. To that extent the family makes the individual less accessible to the more squalid forms of national chauvinism. Those who love their families well will always love the state less. In other words, the family teaches values that are not always consistent with state norms, and for that reason it stands in oppositional complementarity to the state. Which is why totalitarian governments invariably try to undermine the authority of the family. So the school, which is itself a state agency, does not strengthen the family by intruding on its terrain. Granted, the family is not functioning as well as it once did. But by taking over the family's responsibilities, the school removes the possibility of the family's ever restoring its authority. The school needs to recognize that it has its own business to conduct, and it must be exceedingly conservative about taking on "problems" simply because the problems exist.

There is yet another reason why the schools should avoid intervening, as a matter of policy, in every conceivable affliction that burdens our youth. By assuming a programmatic responsibility for a problem, the school automatically transforms it into a *social* problem and thereby lends support to the growing acceptance of the idea of individual powerlessness. Once an institution takes on a problem, to some extent individuals are released from the obligation to solve it themselves. It is true enough that much of the pain and inconvenience of modern life are systemic in their origin and cannot be eliminated without social or political action. It is truer still that many of the inadequacies of our youth are a direct result of social conditions over which they themselves have little or no control—as, for example, the impact of the information environment on them. But it is not true that every difficulty, every inadequacy, every failing, is entirely social in origin and beyond the range of personal control. Although the liberal point of view does not easily admit it, each person has the capability to take responsibility for some part of his or her life, and of altering that which is painful or destructive. It may come as a surprise to some social reformers, but poverty does not necessarily prevent a child from coming to school and paying attention. It is not ineluctably determined by social conditions that a youth will become a drug addict or a bigot or a thief or an ignoramus or a moral idiot or even a chronically unemployable person. "Society" does not make anyone become any of these things, and the schools ought not to encourage the idea that it does. A good teacher, of course, will always be available to talk with students informally about drugs, sex, morality, or anything else that troubles them, and will certainly try to assist a student who has some special difficulty or handicap. A teacher is, after all, an adult as well as a teacher, and in one's efforts to grow up, one needs the help of adults. But it is not necessary for the school to devise "programs" or "curriculum offerings" to deal with every difficulty in life. By doing so, it tends to stress the failures of society and to encourage a sort of "devil made me do it" attitude in the young. In other words, the proliferation of school programs for the disadvantaged and for the disaffected, as well as programs in bilingual education, sex education, drug education, ethnic education, etc., tends to create a psychology of "victimization."[2]

I do not want to be misunderstood on this point. There is no question that economic opportunity and social services need to be improved, and that this must be done at state and federal levels. I am not arguing here for a restoration of the Horatio Alger mythology. But I am saying that schools are, first of all, not prepared to solve these problems; second, that their attempts to do so only weaken the capacity of other institutions; and third, that schools ought not to institute programs which encourage the myth of impotence and victimization.

Below is a short list of some of the "problems" I have in mind which schools have tended to assume responsibility for. Each one is accompanied by a briefly stated opinion about it, the sum of which is that by placing these matters on their agenda, the schools tend toward utopianism and at the same time weaken the power both of other institutions and of individuals.

Sex Education

There is no teaching that attacks more directly the authority of both family and religion than sex education in the schools. Attitudes about sex, as well as the form in which knowledge about sex is communicated, vary from group to group and from family to family. How, when, and where sex education is to take place are among the most important decisions parents must make. Embedded in these decisions are the family's deepest values about the meaning of human relations, which, in turn, usually reflect fundamental religious conceptions. If the school has come up with a definitive view on what is the meaning of sex, and how and when this meaning is to be taught, I have not heard about it. It is sheer insolence, and patronizing insolence at that, that the schools have even proposed to deal with these matters. Of course, it is sometimes explained, by way of justification, that teachers merely provide technical information about reproductive organs. To the extent that such instruction is part of the study of biology, it is obviously essential. But to the extent that such instruction claims to be sex education, it is an equally obvious distortion. If there is one subject whose understanding is not enhanced by mere technical information, I would judge it to be human sexuality. The reduction of sex education to a biological description is, in fact, not sex education at all. Better that it should be done "in the streets," where at least it is filled with emotion, robustness, and flavor. In short, I deny that schools know what a healthy attitude about sex is, or that they have any legitimate claim to preempt religious or family teachings in this matter.

Teaching the Whole Child

To the extent that this unfortunate phrase means that there is more to a child than intellect, it is unquestionably useful. But to the extent that it implies that the school must assume responsibility for every aspect of a child's development, it is self-defeating nonsense. The reasoning usually goes like this: Children cannot learn if they are hungry, emotionally upset, mistreated at home, come from a deprived social class, etc. Therefore, it is foolish to expect much of them until we give them food, psychological counseling, and sufficient emotional sustenance to overcome family psychopathology and social inequities. This is what the school must concentrate on before real learning can take place.

Now, it is certainly possible and necessary to provide children with food when their parents do not or cannot, although school lunches are notorious for their lack of nutritional value—which is to say, the school does not do even this relatively simple task well. This is hardly surprising, since schools are not designed to be commissaries. But feeding children aside, the schools are most emphatically not designed to provide adequate psychological counseling or to provide relief from an oppressive home or an unfair social system. This does not mean that schools cannot be healthy and just environments. It means that we must not expect schools to be psychiatric clinics or teachers to be effective social workers and political reformers. In other words, the schools cannot deal with the "whole child," and it is cruelly misleading for educators to give the impression that they can.

Motivation to Learn

Included in the idea of teaching the whole child is the notion that school can equalize learning opportunities by providing children with motivation to learn. This seems to me an unrealistic notion and, once again, misleading to parents, who may in many cases have come to believe in it. It is true that a teacher who inspires confidence, gives encouragement, and exudes warmth and understanding will facilitate learning. But it is also true that a school cannot provide children with the emotional and social preparation for school learning. Only parents can do this, and when they do not, their children are more than disadvantaged. They are usually disabled. This is often a disaster for children, but the school is simply not organized to justify to the child the value of its teachings or to supply what parents have failed to do. The school provides a service, not a religion. There is some truth in the observation of cynical education critics that those who are successful in school are those who know before they get there what the school will teach them. But in saying this, these critics think they are demeaning the function and quality of schools. They are not. They are merely making the sound observation that motivation, socialization, discipline, and the entire ensemble of attitudes required for success in school are not taught in school. And there is no reason that they should be. A school is not a home. A school teacher is not a parent. Parents have six years in which to prepare and motivate a child. If parents fail, the child usually does, and so does the school.

Ethnic Pride

One of the more insulting usurpations of personal and family authority is the schools' attempt to instill ethnic pride in students. The preservation of, or separation from, one's ethnic or cultural heritage is, it seems to me, essentially a private matter and certainly does not extend beyond the scope of the family. Some people wish to identify themselves with their heritage, some do not, and others sustain a passive curiosity about it. To insist that everyone identify with his or her special group is as impositional and authoritarian as insisting that everyone become a "model American," which, in an earlier time, was one of the goals of the schools. In other words, a state agency which today tries to persuade people to take pride in their blackness, Spanishness, Polishness, or Greekness can, tomorrow, encourage them to abandon such affiliation. Once it has license to do one, it has license to do the other. It goes without saying that the idea of having a special curriculum for an ethnic group or, even worse, having black teachers teach black children, Spanish teachers teach Spanish children, etc., is vile, racist nonsense.

Prayer in the Schools

Those who are distressed by the prohibition of public prayer in the schools sometimes express their grievance by saying that God has been ordered out of the classroom. It is to be wondered what sort of God they have in mind who is stymied by a Supreme Court decision. In any case, consistent with what I have said about ethnic pride and sex education, I do not see it as within the scope of the school to encourage children to practice their religion, or not to. One hopes that every child will come to school with humane ethical conceptions which have been learned at home or in church, and one hopes as well that those who find inspiration or comfort in prayer will have sufficient opportunity to exercise this right in their homes or at church or wherever else they have a moment of peace—including the study hall, gym, and English class, where typically, intellectual activity is at a minimum. But to make prayer part of the school's program is to implicate the school in a realm which it has no business to enter.

Psychotherapy

That reason, as Plato remarked, must have an emotional base can hardly be denied. But that schools ought to provide systematic "emotional" education certainly can be denied. Of course, in an informal way, every teacher must confront the emotions of a student. But I do not know what is the source of authority by which schools institute programs in transcendental meditation, Rolfing, est, or any other "therapy," including what are called "rap sessions." In the first place, like so many other undertakings that go beyond the competence of school personnel, therapeutic education is rarely done proficiently. In the second place, it has by no means been established that any of these procedures are "effective." It is at least an open question as to whether they do more harm than good. In the third place, there is no therapy of which I am aware, including the Rogerian, that does not have a particular philosophic bias with which the students, their parents, or their religion might disagree. This bias is rarely made explicit, and therefore the practice of any form of psychotherapy in the schools is impositional and possibly dishonest.

In spite of the dogmatic tone I have taken in stating them, the opinions above are offered only as examples of how I think the forming of a school's agenda ought to be approached—that is, with skepticism and restraint. There may, for example, be arguments in favor of sex education or prayer or ethnic propaganda that I have overlooked and with which, in the end, I might concur. But such arguments would have to be of almost transcendent significance before admitting them. The point I am making is that the schools ought to resist, not welcome, assuming responsibilities that failing communities or people seem only too willing to hand over to them. The school must acknowledge that in almost every instance where it has tried to do what the family, the church, the economy, or the political system has failed to do, it has also failed, and at the expense of doing well what it is best suited to do. It would, in fact, be an enormous impetus to more effective schooling if the curriculum of every school specified not only what will be taught but what will *not* be taught. How refreshing it would be, and how liberating, to find a school that publicly declared that it has designed an educational program from which children will *not* learn, among other things, to love God, to be proud that they are Greeks, to save money, to be tender lovers, to be free of guilt, and to avoid misusing drugs. The list of what such a school would not do would naturally be three or four times the length of the list of what it could. However, the longer list might be accompanied by a statement to the effect that the school certainly does not oppose such learnings. And it might even specify which social institutions are responsible for which of the learnings. Freed of utopian dreams and the IFD disease, the school could then get down to its proper business. And it is to that subject that I want now to turn.

ISBN: 0-440-08651-5

Some
Solutions

7
Redefining
Relevance

During most of the 1960s and early 1970s the word that received the heaviest pounding in discourses on education was "relevance." Every education writer, it seemed, was expected to work it over thoroughly, and I joined in the fun myself in at least two books I wrote. The prevailing opinion, in those years, was that educational relevance meant that which has a bearing on a student's life in some direct and urgent way. It followed from this that any topic that was relevant would engage the student's wholehearted attention and by that sole virtue was deserving of inclusion in the school curriculum. The opposite was also held to be true: That which did not have a direct and urgent bearing on a student's life was mere pedantry and a waste of valuable time.

The question of what "having a bearing" meant was not gone into, at least not deeply. History, for example, was usually found not to qualify. It was assumed that since we lived amidst revolutionary conditions, the experience of the past could not have a bearing, an assumption which students daily amplified by displaying a measure of disdain toward events that had not occurred during the lifetime of the Beatles. Many of them, I imagine, still feel this way.

History was not the only subject to take a beating at the hands of relevance, especially in high school and college. Science, music, art, foreign languages, and literature came under the closest scrutiny by being put to the "direct and urgent" test. In literature, for example, it could be demonstrated that Shakespeare, Milton, Dickens, Poe, and Melville, to name a few, were irrelevant because they had not addressed themselves either to the causes of the Viet Nam War or to American racism. Besides, their sentence structure, vocabulary, and references were not immediately accessible to the reader. Accordingly, it was held that Lorraine Hansberry, Kurt Vonnegut, Ray Bradbury, and Bob Dylan would do quite nicely as replacements. The point is that in every subject where it was possible to do so, that which was most contemporary, familiar, and controversial was brought to the forefront. Relevance meant "now." Just like television.

From our present vantage point it is easy to ridicule this conception of relevance, especially for its crudeness and superficiality. But I think it fair to point out that in the circumstances that produced it, it was not entirely unjustified. In many schools traditional subjects were taught, and are still, in such an uninspired and even meaningless way that almost anything is preferable to their deadening influence. Moreover, it is certainly true that a student can sometimes be led to a disciplined study of enduring subjects through the stimulus provided by an interest of the moment. And we must not forget that through most of the years to which I am referring there was a war in progress. People were being killed, for reasons that were anything but clear. The times were nervous and tormenting, and there arose a passionate and honest doubting of the value of traditional academics amidst all the carnage and confusion. But now, the times are not so nervous, and still less tormenting. We may be permitted to reconsider the question of what relevance means, or, more to the point, what has a bearing on a student's life.

From everything I have written so far, you will guess that my answer begins in this way: What has the most relevance to students is that which the information environment least provides them. To leave the students entirely to the dominant biases of the culture is to guarantee them a one-dimensional education and a half-developed personality; one leaves them, as it were, to the mercies of the media, the technocrats, the utopians. What is relevant, therefore, is what the culture is insisting is irrelevant. I have contended, for example, that the media curriculum is image-centered, and in an insidious way inimical to linguistic expression. That is why I shall devote the next two chapters to language education in the schools, and will say something about it in this chapter. An information environment which does not stress language and language development must be countered by an education that does. But I have also argued that the media curriculum is, among other things, discontinuous in its content, immediate in its gratifications, present-centered, and nonanalytical. And I have argued further that the Technical Thesis undermines the authority of human judgment and that the Utopian Thesis tends to stress the impotence of individual responsibility.

It follows from all this that the schooling of our youth must provide the opposite of, or at least an alternative to, these biases. This chapter, then, is an attempt to redefine educational relevance as a corrective to the burdens of cultural bias. All of the remaining chapters in the book have this as their purpose, as well.

In consideration of the powerful teachings of the media, perhaps the most important contribution schools can make to the education of our youth is to provide them with a sense of coherence in their studies; that is, a sense of purpose, meaning, and interconnectedness in what they learn. At present a typical modern school curriculum reflects, far too much, the fragmentation one finds in television's weekly schedule. Each subject, like each program, has nothing whatever to do with any other and for reasons that are even less justifiable than the reasons for television's discontinuity and incoherence. We must say this for television: It offers what it does in the hope of winning the student's attention. Its major theme is the psychological gratification of the viewer. Schools, on the other hand, offer what they do either because they have always done so or because the colleges or professional schools "require" it. There is no longer any principle that unifies the school curriculum and furnishes it with meaning.

A notable exception to this is found in some religious schools, where subjects are selected and taught with a view toward developing the moral sensibility of students, as this is understood by adherents of a particular religion. I have before me, as an example, an account of the efforts of twenty Fundamentalist schools in Kentucky to keep themselves apart from the regulations of the Kentucky State Board of Education.[1] Among other things, these schools do not wish to use state-approved textbooks because such books either ignore or discredit the Biblical version of Creation. But even more important, state curriculum requirements would undermine the religious theme of *all* subjects taught in Fundamentalist schools. The argument, as expressed by Reverend C. C. Hinton of Somerset, Kentucky, is that religion "is not offered as a course or as a separate part of the curriculum. It is permeated into all parts of the curriculum." Though his grammar may be shaky, Reverend Hinton's belief in the beneficent and binding influence of religious principle is firm. He is obviously an educator, not a technocrat, which is to say, he has some conception of what an education might be for.

I am, of course, not recommending Fundamentalism to

anyone, or Catholicism, which also provides a unifying religious theme in its educational program. But I do suggest that modern secular education fails in its obligation to be relevant because it has no moral, social, or intellectual center. There is no set of ideas or attitudes that "is permeated into all parts of the curriculum." The curriculum is not, in fact, a "course of study" at all but a meaningless hodgepodge of subjects. It does not even put forward a clear vision of what constitutes an educated person, except if it is, as "back to the basics" would have it, a person who possesses "skills." In other words, a technocrat's ideal—a person with no commitment and no point of view but with plenty of marketable skills. If, in fact, there is at present any underlying theme to American education it is precisely that: Education is to provide jobs. It has no purpose other than as preparation for entrance into the economy.

I believe it is this emptiness of moral, social, and even intellectual motivation and meaning, not only in our schools but in our culture, that provoked Aleksandr Solzhenitsyn's grim critique of America in his much publicized speech at Harvard in June 1978. It is the same emptiness that Yeats wrote about sixty years before when, in "The Second Coming," he told us that the center cannot hold and that mere anarchy is loosed upon the world. Yeats's solution is unclear (at least to me) and Solzhenitsyn's—a militant anticommunism—has been tried, and it failed to take hold. Nonetheless it cannot be doubted that some transcendent and binding point of view about learning is necessary in our present situation.

Of course, we must not overestimate the capability of the schools to provide such a point of view in the face of a culture in which almost all coherence seems to have disappeared. In our technicalized, present-centered information environment, it is not easy to locate a rationale for education, let alone impart one convincingly. It is obvious, for example, that the schools cannot restore religion to the center of the life of learning. With the exception, perhaps, of a few people in Somerset, Kentucky, no one would take seriously the idea that learning is for the greater glory of God. It is equally obvious that the knowledge explosion has blown apart the feasibility of such limited but coordinated curriculums as, for example, the trivium and quadrivium. Or even a Great Books curriculum. There are some people—more quiet than once they were—who would have us stress love of country as a unifying principle in education. Experience has shown, however, that this invariably translates into love of government, and in practice becomes indistinguishable from what is at the center of Soviet or Chinese education.

There are some who would put forward "emotional health" as the core of the curriculum. I refer here to that point of view sometimes called Rogerian, sometimes Maslovian, which stresses above all else the development of one's emotional life through the quest for one's "real self." Such an idea, of course, renders a curriculum irrelevant since only "self-knowledge," i.e., one's feelings, is considered worthwhile. Carl Rogers himself has said that anything that can be taught is probably either trivial or harmful, thus making any discussion of the schools unnecessary. But beyond this, the culture is already so heavy with the burden of the glorification of "self" that it would be redundant to have the schools stress it, even if it were possible. There is also the question of whether or not a preoccupation with exploring "interior space" would produce a generation of ignoramuses. From what I have been able to observe, current advocates of this version of "humanist" philosophy seem to have retreated into a curious kind of self-centeredness which finds satisfaction in ESP, astrology, and Eastern mysticism. Their search for themselves appears to exclude an awareness of everyone else.

One obviously treads on shaky ground in suggesting a

plausible theme for a diverse, secularized population. Nonetheless, with all due apprehension, I would propose as a possibility the theme which animates Jacob Bronowski's *The Ascent of Man.* It is a book, and a philosophy, filled with optimism and suffused with the transcendent belief that humanity's destiny is the discovery of knowledge. Moreover, although Bronowski's emphasis is on science, he finds ample warrant to include the arts and humanities as part of our unending quest to gain a unified understanding of nature and our place in it.

Thus, to chart the ascent of man, which I will here call "the ascent of humanity," we must join art and science. But we must also join the past and the present, for the ascent of humanity is above all a continuous story. It is, in fact, a story of creation, although not quite the one that the Fundamentalists fight so fiercely to defend. It is the story of humanity's creativeness in trying to conquer loneliness, ignorance, and disorder. And it certainly includes the development of various religious systems as a means of providing order and meaning to existence. In this context it is inspiring to note that the Biblical version of creation, to the astonishment of everyone except possibly the Fundamentalists, has turned out to be a near-perfect blend of artistic imagination and scientific intuition: the Big Bang theory of the creation of the universe, now widely accepted by cosmologists, confirms in essential details what the Bible proposes as having been the case "in the beginning."

In any event, the virtues of adopting the ascent of humanity as a scaffolding on which to build a curriculum are many and various, especially in our present situation. For one thing, with a few exceptions which I shall note, it does not require that we invent new subjects or discard old ones. The structure of the subject-matter curriculum which presently exists in most schools is entirely usable. For another, it is a theme which can begin in the earliest grades and extend through college in ever-deepening and widening dimensions. Better still, it provides students with a point of view from which to understand the meaning of subjects, for each subject can be seen as a battleground of sorts, an area in which fierce intellectual struggle has taken place and continues to take place. Each idea within a subject marks the place where someone fell and someone rose. Thus, the ascent of humanity is an optimistic story, not without its miseries but dominated by astonishing and repeated victories. From this point of view, the curriculum itself may be seen as a celebration of human intelligence and creativity, not a meaningless collection of diploma or college requirements.

But best of all, the theme of the ascent of humanity provides us with a nontechnical, noncommercial definition of education. It is a definition drawn from an honorable humanistic tradition and reflects a concept of the purposes of academic life that goes counter to the biases of the technocrats, the utopians, and the media. I am referring to the idea that to become educated means to become aware of the origins and growth of knowledge and knowledge systems; to be familiar with the intellectual and creative processes by which the best that has been thought and said has been produced; to learn how to participate, even if as a listener, in what Robert Maynard Hutchins once called The Great Conversation, which is merely a different metaphor for what is meant by the ascent of humanity. You will note that such a definition is not child-centered, not training-centered, not skill-centered, not even problem-centered. It is idea-centered and coherence-centered. It is also otherworldly, in the sense that it does not assume that what one learns in school must be directly and urgently related to a problem of today. In other words, it is an education that stresses history, the scientific mode of thinking, the disciplined use of language, a wide-ranging knowledge of the arts and religion, and the continuity of human enterprise. It is a definition of education that provides an excellent corrective to the antihistorical, nonanalytical, nonsequential, immediately gratifying biases of the present information environment.

Let us consider history first, for it is in some ways the central discipline in all of this. It is hardly necessary for me to argue here that, as Cicero put it, "To remain ignorant of things that happened before you were born is to remain a child." It is enough to say that history is our most potent intellectual means of achieving a "raised consciousness." But there are some points about history and its teaching that require stressing since they are usually ignored by our schools. The first is that history is not merely one subject among many that may be taught in school. Every subject has a history, including biology, physics, mathematics, literature, music, and art. As I shall propose in the next chapter that every teacher must be a language teacher, I would propose here that every teacher must be a history teacher. To teach, for example, what we know about biology today without also teaching what we once knew, or thought we knew, is to reduce knowledge to a mere consumer product. It is to deprive students of a sense of the meaning of what we know, and of how we know. To teach about the atom without Democritus, to teach about electricity without Faraday, to teach about political science without Aristotle or Machiavelli, to teach about music without Haydn, is to refuse our students access to The Great Conversation. It is to deny them knowledge of their roots, about which no other social institution is presently concerned. For to know about your roots is not merely to know where your grandfather came from, and what he had to endure. It is also to know where your ideas come from, and why you happen to believe them; and to know where your moral and aesthetic sensibility comes from. It is to know where your world, not just your family, comes from. To complete Cicero's thought, begun above: "What is a human life worth unless it is incorporated into the lives of one's ancestors and set in an historical context?" By "ancestors" Cicero did not mean your mother's aunt.

Thus, I would recommend that every subject be taught *as* history. In this way, children, even in the earliest grades, can begin to understand, as they presently do not, that knowledge is not a fixed thing but a stage in human development, with a past and a future. To return for a moment to theories of creation, we want to be able to show how an idea conceived almost four thousand years ago has traveled not only in time but in meaning, from science to religious metaphor to science again. What a lovely and profound coherence there is in the connection between the wonderous speculations in an ancient Hebrew desert tent and the equally wonderous speculations in a modern MIT classroom! What I am trying to say is that the history of subjects teaches connections; it teaches that the world is not created anew each day, that everyone stands on someone else's shoulders.

I am well aware that this approach to subjects would be difficult to use. There are, at present, few texts that would help very much, and teachers have not, in any case, been prepared to know about knowledge in this way. Moreover, there is the added difficulty of our learning how to do this for children of different ages. But that it needs to be done is, in my opinion, beyond question.

The teaching of subjects as studies in historical continuities is not intended to make history as a special subject irrelevant. If every subject is taught with an historical dimension, the history teacher would be free to teach what histories are; which is to say, hypotheses and theories about why change occurs. There is a sense in which there is no such thing as "history," for every historian, from Thucydides to Toynbee, has known that his stories must be told from a special point of view which always reflects a particular theory of social development. And historians also know that they write histories for some particular purpose. More often than not, either to glorify or condemn the present. Thus, there is no definitive history of anything; there are only histories, human inventions which do not give us *the* answers, but give us only those answers called forth by the particular questions that were asked.

Historians know all of this—it is a commonplace idea among them. Yet it is kept a secret from our youth. Their ignorance of it prevents them from understanding how "history" can change and why the Russians, Chinese, American Indians, and virtually everyone else see historical events differently from the authors of history schoolbooks.

The task of the history teacher, then, is to become a "histories teacher." This does not mean that some particular version of the American, European, or Asian past should remain untold. A student who does not know at least one history is in no position to evaluate others. But it does mean that a histories teacher will be concerned, at all times, to show how histories are themselves a product of culture; how any history is a mirror of the conceits and even metaphysical biases of the culture that produces it; how the religion, politics, geography, and economy of a people lead them to recreate their past along certain lines. The histories teacher must clarify for students the meaning of "objectivity" and "events," must show what a "point of view" and a "theory" are, must provide some sense of how histories may be evaluated.

It will be objected that this idea—history as comparative history—is too abstract for students to grasp. But this is one of several reasons why comparative history should be taught. To teach the past simply as a chronicle of indisputable, fragmented, and concrete events is to replicate the bias of the media, which largely deny our youth access to concepts and theories, and provide them only with a stream of meaningless events. That is why the controversies that develop around what events ought to be included in the "history" curriculum have a somewhat hollow ring to them. Some people urge, for example, that the Holocaust, or Stalin's bloodbaths, or the trail of Indian tears be taught in school. I agree that our students should know about such things but we must still address the question, What is it that we want them to "know" about these events? Are they to be explained as the "maniac" theory of history? Are they to be understood as illustrations of the "banality of evil" or the "law of survival?" Are they manifestations of the universal force of economic greed? Are they examples of human nature?

Whatever events may be included in the study of the past, the worst thing we can do is to present them devoid of the coherence that a theory or theories can provide; that is to say, as meaningless. This, we can be sure, the media do daily. The histories teacher must go far beyond the "event" level into the realm of concepts, theories, hypotheses, comparisons, deductions, evaluations. In other words, the idea is to raise the level of abstraction at which "history" is taught. This idea would apply to all subjects, including science.

From the point of view of the ascent of humanity, the scientific enterprise is one of our most glorious achievements. On humanity's Judgment Day we can be expected to speak first of our science. I have already stressed the importance of teaching the history of science in every science course but this is no more important than teaching its "philosophy." I mention this with some sense of despair. More than half the high schools in the United States do not even offer one course in physics.[2] And at a rough guess, I would estimate that in ninety percent of the schools chemistry is still taught as if students were being trained to be druggists. To suggest, therefore, that science is an exercise in human imagination, that it is something quite different from technology, that there are "philosophies" of science, and that all of this ought to form part of a scientific education, is to feel oneself to be ridiculous. But I believe it nonetheless.

Would it be an exaggeration to say that not one student in fifty knows what "induction" means? Or knows what a scientific theory is? Or a scientific model? Or knows what are the optimum conditions of a valid scientific experiment? Or has ever considered the question of what scientific truth is? In *The Identity of Man* Bronowski says the following: "This is the paradox of imagination in science, that it has for its aim the impoverishment of imagination. By that outrageous phrase, I mean that the highest flight of scientific imagination is to weed out the proliferation of new ideas. In science, the grand view is a miserly view, and a rich model of the universe is one which is as poor as possible in hypotheses."

Is there one student in a hundred who can make any sense out of this statement? Though the phrase "impoverishment of imagination" may be outrageous, there is nothing startling or even unusual about the idea contained in this quotation. Every practicing scientist understands what Bronowski is saying. Yet it is kept a secret from our students. It should be revealed. In addition to each particular science course including a serious historical dimension, I would propose that every school—elementary through college—offer and require a course in the philosophy of science. Such a course should include a consideration of the language of science, the nature of scientific proof, the source of scientific hypotheses, the role of imagination, the conditions of experimentation, and especially the value of error and disproof. If I am not mistaken, there are still many people who believe that what makes a statement scientific is that it can be verified. In fact exactly the opposite is the case: What separates scientific statements from nonscientific statements is that the former can be falsified and the latter cannot. What makes science possible is not our ability to recognize "truth" but our ability to recognize falsehood.

What such a course would try to get at is the notion that science is not pharmacy or technology or magic tricks but a special way of employing human intelligence. It would be important for students to learn that one does not become scientific by donning a white coat (which is what television teaches) but by practicing a set of canons of thought, many of which have to do with the disciplined use of language. "The method of scientific investigation," Thomas Henry Huxley wrote, "is nothing but the expression of the necessary mode of working of the human mind." What he meant is that science involves a method of employing language that is accessible to everyone. The ascent of humanity has rested largely on that fact.

I shall be saying more about the role of language in the formation of knowledge in the next chapter. But here, on the subject of the disciplined use of language, I should like to propose that, in addition to courses in the philosophy of science, every school—again, from elementary school through college—offer a course in semantics—in the processes by which people make meaning. In this connection I must note the gloomy fact that English teachers have been consistently obtuse in their approach to this subject, which is to say, they have largely ignored it. This has always been difficult for me to understand in light of the fact that English teachers claim to be concerned to teach reading and writing. But if they do not teach anything about the relationship of language to reality—which is what semantics studies—I cannot imagine how they expect reading and writing to improve.

Every teacher ought to be a semantics teacher since it is not possible to separate language from what we call knowledge. Like history, semantics is an interdisciplinary subject: It is necessary to know something about it in order to understand any subject. But it would be extremely useful to the growth of their intelligence if our youth had available a special course in which fundamental principles of language were identified and explained. Such a course would deal not only with the various uses of language but with the relationship between things and words, symbols and signs, factual statements and judgments, and grammar and thought. Especially for young students, the course ought to emphasize the kinds of semantic errors that are common to all of us, and which are avoidable through awareness and discipline. I refer here to such tendencies as the use of either-or categories, misunderstanding of levels of abstraction, confusion of words with things, sloganeering, and self-reflexiveness. Fortunately, there are many books available for use as a text in such a course—from first grade through college.[3]

Of all the disciplines that might be included in the curriculum, semantics is certainly among the most "basic." Because it deals with the processes by which we make and interpret meaning, it has great potential for affecting the deepest levels of student intelligence. And yet semantics is rarely mentioned when "back to the basics" is proposed. Why? My guess is that it cuts too deep. To borrow from George Orwell, many subjects are basic but some are more basic than others. They have the capability of generating critical thought and of giving students access to questions that get to the heart of the matter. This is not what "back to the basics" advocates usually have in mind. They want language technicians: people who can follow instructions, write reports clearly, spell correctly. Instruction in semantics tends to achieve some of this. There is certainly ample evidence that the study of semantics will improve the writing and reading of students. But it invariably does more. It helps students to reflect on the sense and truth of what they are writing and of what they are asked to read. It teaches them to discover the underlying assumptions of what they are told. It emphasizes the manifold ways in which language can distort reality. It assists students in becoming what Charles Weingartner and I once called "crap-detectors." Students who have a firm grounding in semantics are therefore apt to find it difficult to take reading tests. A reading test does not invite one to ask whether or not what is written is true. Or if it is true, what it has to do with anything. The study of semantics insists upon these questions. But "back to the basics" advocates don't require education to be *that* basic. Which is why they usually do not include literature, music, and art as part of their agenda either. But of course in using the ascent of humanity as a theme, we would of necessity elevate such subjects to prominence.

The most obvious reason for such prominence is that their subject matter contains the best evidence we have of the unity and continuity of human experience and feeling. And that is why I would propose that in our teaching of the humanities, we should emphasize the enduring creations of the past. Except under conditions I will discuss in Chapter Ten, the schools should stay as far from contemporary works as possible. Because of the nature of the communications industry, our students have continuous access to the popular arts of their own times—its music, rhetoric, design, literature, architecture. Their knowledge of the form and content of this art is by no means satisfactory. But their ignorance of the form and content of the art of the past is cavernous. This is one good reason for emphasizing the art of the past. Another is that there is no subject better suited to freeing us from the tyranny of the present than the historical study of art. Painting, for example, is more than three times as old as writing, and contains in its changing styles and themes a fifteen-thousand-year-old record of the ascent of humanity.

In saying this, I do not mean to subsume art under the heading of archeology, although I should certainly recommend that the history of art forms be given a serious place in the curriculum. But art is much more than an historical artifact. To have meaning for us, it must connect with those levels of feeling that are in fact not expressible in discursive language. And the question arises, Is it possible for students of today to relate, through feeling, to the painting, architecture, music, sculpture, or literature of the past? The answer, I believe, is: only with the greatest difficulty. They, and many of us, have an aesthetic sensibility of a different order from what is required to be inspired, let alone entertained, by a Shakespeare sonnet, a Haydn symphony, or a Hals painting. To oversimplify the matter, a young man who believes the Led Zeppelin to have reached the highest pinnacle of musical expression lacks the sensibility to distinguish between the ascent and descent of humanity. But that is an oversimplification, and in any case it is not my intention to further blacken the reputation of popular culture. The point I want to make is that the products of the popular arts are amply provided by the First Curriculum. The Second Curriculum must make available the products of classical art forms precisely because they are not so available and because they demand a different order of sensibility and response. In our present circumstances, there is no excuse for schools to sponsor rock concerts when students have not heard the music of Mozart, Beethoven, Bach, or Chopin. Or for students to have graduated from high school without having read, for example, Shakespeare, Milton, Keats, Dickens, Whitman, Twain, Melville, or Poe. Or for students not to have seen at least a photograph of paintings by Goya, El Greco, David. It is not to the point that many of these composers, writers, and painters were in their own times popular artists. What is to the point is that they spoke, when they did, in a language and from a point of view different from our own and yet continuous with our own. These artists are relevant not only because they established the standards with which civilized people approach the arts. They are relevant because the First Curriculum tries to mute their voices and render their standards invisible.

It is highly likely that students, immersed in today's popular arts, will find such an emphasis as I suggest tedious and even painful. This fact will, in turn, be painful to teachers who, naturally enough, prefer to teach that which will arouse an immediate and enthusiastic response. But our youth must be shown that not all worthwhile things are instantly accessible and that there are levels of sensibility unknown to them. Above all, they must be shown humanity's artistic roots. And that task, in our own times, falls inescapably on the schools.

On the subject of roots, I want to end this chapter by including in my definition of educational relevance the subject of religion, with which so much of our painting, music, architecture, literature, *and* science is intertwined. Specifically, I want to propose that the curriculum include a course in comparative religion. Such a course would deal with religion as an expression of humanity's creativeness; that is, as a total, integrated response to fundamental questions about the meaning of existence. The course would be descriptive, promoting no particular religion but illuminating the metaphors, the literature, the art, the ritual of religious expression itself. I am not unaware of the difficulties such a course would face, not the least of which is the belief that the schools and religion must on no account touch each other. But I do not see how we can claim to be educating our youth if we do not ask them to consider how different people of different times and places have tried to achieve a sense of transcendence. No conserving education can neglect such sacred texts as Genesis, the New Testament, the Koran, the Bhagavad-Gita. Each of them embodies a style and a world view which tell as much about the ascent of humanity as any book ever written. To these books I would add the *Communist Manifesto,* since I think it reasonable to classify it as a sacred text, embodying religious principles to which millions of people are devoted.

To summarize: I am proposing, as a beginning, a curriculum in which all subjects are presented as a stage in humanity's historical development; in which the philosophies of science, of history, of language, and of religion are taught; and in which there is a strong emphasis on classical forms of artistic expression. This is a curriculum, in other words, that goes "back to the basics," although not quite the way the technocrats mean it.

8
Language Education in a Knowledge Context

As I write, the largest city in the United States has just taken on a new head of its schools. Among his first substantive public statements—it may even have been his first—was the announcement of a program of incentives for schools that can improve their students' reading scores. As worldly people, we understand that heads of school systems must make statements of popular appeal, but in this instance there is little doubt about the earnestness of Chancellor Frank Macchiarola of New York City. He has indicated in several ways, among which prizes are but one, that his administration will be committed, first and foremost, to the improvement of reading scores, and *not,* please note, to the improvement of reading, which is another matter altogether.

The improvement of reading scores is, in fact, a quite simple goal to achieve. There are several ways to do it, by far the best being to provide students with the official reading test three days before they must take it. The most effective way to do well on a test is to know what the exact questions will be and to make sure you know their answers. In education this is sometimes called reviewing for a test. To borrow from Dr. Johnson, the availability of a test before it is given wonderfully concentrates the mind.

However, for reasons that are not as clear to me as to others of finer ethics, this procedure is generally regarded as dishonest, in which case an alternative method would be to provide students with reading tests that are similar in content and form to the test they will actually take. They may, then, do these tests in class and at home every week for, say, ten weeks prior to the "official test." In this way students will not learn very much about reading, but they are likely to learn a great deal about taking reading tests. Their scores will improve. Their schools will win such awards as Mr. Macchiarola has promised. And *The New York Times* will have a first page story to lift our spirits. The students will still be disabled as readers, but their burden will recede as a public issue. As previously noted, technical people are apt to be preoccupied with scores, not competence, which is probably why Mr. Macchiarola offered no incentives for the improvement of speaking and listening. There are no generally accepted standardized tests for producing a speaking or listening score, and Mr. Macchiarola is undoubtedly a product of the Admiral Hyman Rickover school of thought which claims that what we need most of all in education are scores. If we cannot get a score for something, we are, like a submarine with neither radar nor radio, lost at sea. It does not matter that our students speak badly and listen worse. Or write as if English were a foreign tongue. If we cannot get a score for these behaviors, we may safely ignore them, or at least we shall offer no incentives to improve them.

In this way of thinking, Mr. Macchiarola and Admiral Rickover have it wrong, of course, and they have it wrong on at least two counts. The first is that the improvement of reading scores is not, in any sense, a legitimate educational goal, and in my opinion it is shocking that so many people accept it as such. I shall deal more carefully with this point in the chapter on evaluation, but I wish to assert here that reading abilities (it is plural, not singular) are not and cannot be measured by the techniques presently used to produce a reading score. The sort of technicalization represented by such procedures demeans our concepts of learning, intelligence, and language, not to mention reading itself. The second mistake, following inexorably from the first, lies in the indifference a "score" mentality displays toward writing, speaking, listening, question-asking, and other manifestations of human intelligence. Although the improvement of reading abilities ought to be a constant goal of the schools, such abilities are no more important than other modes of linguistic expression and are, in fact, inseparable from them.

From everything you have read in this book so far, you will properly conclude that, in the face of the nonlinguistic information bias of our culture, I would propose that the schools place the strongest possible emphasis on language education. But it is necessary to stress at the outset that this cannot be done by mentalities that view language behaviors as scores or even as "skills." Those who conceive of language in this way have little to offer us except a kind of vocational or at least mechanical approach to the subject in the form of exercises, assignments, and tests. They eventually get around to proposing "more grammar" as a way of accomplishing their ends, which, sad to say, it never does. We do not know nearly as much as we should about how children learn language, but if there is one thing we can say with assurance it is that knowledge of grammatical nomenclature and skill in sentence-parsing have no bearing whatsoever on the process.[1] The teaching of grammar is both the first and the last refuge of the educational technocrat. It is his natural inclination to think of all learning as modeled on driver education; that is to say, he believes language competence consists of one's being in command of an ensemble of mechanical skills, all of which lie outside of our personalities, our purposes, and our knowledge. I am here arguing the opposite: Of all things to be learned, in school or out, languaging, as I prefer to call the process, is least like a mechanical skill. It is, in fact, the most intimate, integrated, emotion-laden learning we do. At no point can we separate what we know and what we are from how our linguistic powers develop, and I would even include in the phrase "linguistic powers" the learning of such matters as spelling, grammar, and punctuation.

People do not speak or write well because they know the mechanics of their language. They know the mechanics of their language because they speak or write well. By this I mean that improved language behavior originates in the deepest need to express one's personality and knowledge, and to do so with variety, control, and precision. Once such a need has been aroused and cultivated, the resources of language, including its mechanics, become objects of intense interest and are apt to be both satisfying and easy to grasp. This is one of several lessons we may learn from the work of Sylvia Ashton-Warner, Paolo Friere, Herbert Kohl, and others who, in successfully teaching children and adults to read and write with intelligently directed purpose, have seen so clearly that language education involves the transformation of personality.[2] To speak new words in new ways is not a cosmetic activity. It is a way of becoming a new person. It involves learning new things and seeing the world in new ways. "A name," Socrates said, "is an instrument of teaching and of distinguishing natures." Twenty-three hundred years later Bertrand Russell made the same point: "Language serves not only to express thought but to make possible thoughts which could not exist without it." What this means is that language education is almost entirely irrelevant when conducted at the level of vocabulary lists, spelling tests, and grammar exercises. Languaging, knowing, and living are intertwined, and it is never easy to know in what ways, if any, they may be distinguished from one another. But this much is clear: Language learning is extremely serious business. A young man whose range of response to that which displeases him is located somewhere between the word "bullshit" and some other unoriginal obscenity does not simply have a vocabulary deficiency. He has a perception deficiency. He cannot distinguish among degrees or kinds of displeasure. The world may be said to be a blur to him, and it is not sufficient to provide him with a vocabulary list. He must somehow have his consciousness raised. He must be persuaded that he is missing something, that there is value, for him, in seeing what is now hidden from his view. Having achieved some sense of what there is to see, he will then require the words, perhaps demand the words, with which to understand and express a wider field of vision.

But at the same time, words may themselves be the agent through which his consciousness is raised. If they appear on a vocabulary list, they surely will not. But if they appear in a context which is filled with importance, if not urgency, they may arouse the sense of curiosity or wonder or need from which durable and profound learning originates.

Words increase our understanding, and our understanding increases our words. We are here in the presence of a transactional relationship which cannot be ignored in planning the language education of our youth. Neither can we ignore what some people call the tyranny of words. For a young man whose emotions are aroused in entirely predictable ways by such words as "democracy" or "racist" or "communism" or "Burger King" may in fact be said to have a vocabulary problem, although not of the sort that education technocrats acknowledge. His "vocabulary problem" is that he is living under the direction of someone else's commands. The words are not fully his. He conducts himself at the sufferance of another.

It may come as a surprise to our technocrat philosophers, but people do not read, write, speak, or listen primarily for the purpose of achieving a test score. They use language in order to conduct their lives, and to control their lives, and to understand their lives. An improvement in one's languaging abilities is therefore not measurable by a vocabulary test or some such HAGOTHian instrument. It is to be observed in changes in one's purposes, perceptions, and evaluations. Language education, at its best, may achieve what George Bernard Shaw asserted is the function of art. "Art," he said in *Quintessence of Ibsenism,* "should refine our sense of character and conduct, of justice and sympathy, greatly heightening our self-knowledge, self-control, precision of action and considerateness, and making us intolerant of baseness, cruelty, injustice, and intellectual superficiality and vulgarity."

Although there is more than a touch of utopianism in it, this is a quotation worth remembering, since it expresses a profound and, one might even say, basic conception of the function of all education, as Shaw knew very well. For my purposes, if you replace the word "art" with the phrase "language education," you will have a precise statement of what I have been trying to say. Nothing short of a conception something like this is going to have much effect on the intelligence and character of children who live in a world of instantaneous, nonhistorical, nonlineal visual imagery.

From this point of view, language learning becomes the central preoccupation of a conserving education, wherein every teacher, regardless of level or subject, must be a language educator. This idea is certainly not a new one, although it has often been interpreted to mean merely that each teacher should take responsibility for correcting students' papers. What I have in mind goes far beyond this.

Let us begin, for example, with question-asking. I would expect very little resistance to the claim that in the development of intelligence nothing can be more "basic" than learning how to ask productive questions. Many years ago, in *Teaching as a Subversive Activity,* Charles Weingartner and

I expressed our astonishment at the neglect shown in school toward this language art. Such neglect continues to astonish. The "back to the basics" philosophers rarely mention it, and practicing teachers usually do not find room for it in their curriculums. Thus, I find it necessary to repeat two obvious facts about question-asking. The first is that all our knowledge results from questions, which is another way of saying that question-asking is our most important intellectual tool. I would go so far as to say that the answers we carry about in our heads are largely meaningless unless we know the questions which produced them. The second fact is that questions are language. To put it simply, a question is a sentence. Badly formed, it produces no knowledge and no understanding. Aptly formed, it leads to new facts, new perspectives, new ideas. As Francis Bacon put it more than three hundred fifty years ago, "There arises from a bad and unapt formation of words a wonderful obstruction to the mind." In other words, stupidity. Let us, then, go "back to Bacon," and make the study of the art of question-asking one of the central disciplines in language education.

Every teacher would then, at all times, be concerned with this discipline. What, for example, are the sorts of questions that obstruct the mind, or free it, in the study of history? How are these questions different from those one might ask of a mathematical proof, or a literary work, or a biological theory? If we are talking about how, in an information environment which does not encourage reflection or analysis, our schools can promote a predisposition to the former and competence in the latter, then the history teacher, the mathematics teacher, the literature teacher, the biology teacher, must show the young how questions are productively formed in speaking their subject, in listening to their subject, in reading their subject. If this or anything like it is presently being done, I have not heard about it. But this I can say for sure: There are at present no reading tests anywhere that measure the ability of students to address probing questions to the particular texts they are reading. Does Admiral Rickover want reading scores? Well perhaps, after all, we may give him some. Let us make up tests that assess the ability of students to put intelligent questions to their texts. The problem, of course, is that such tests would not be easy to grade, since the grading of them would be as much a measure of those who are doing the assessment as of those who are being assessed.

In any event we must not talk of tests but of serious matters. What I am saying is that to study a subject is to enter a particular language environment. What students need to know are the rules of discourse which comprise the subject, and among the most central of such rules are those which govern what is and what is not a legitimate question. I do not intend here to produce a textbook on the art of asking questions or to specify the rules of questioning in different subjects (neither of which tasks I am smart enough to perform). But it is possible to indicate two concepts that are central to the process of question-asking and which must form part of a basic language education. The first is suggested by a charming story attributed to the psychologist Gordon Allport: Two priests, it seems, were engaged in a dispute on whether or not it is permissible to pray and smoke at the same time. One believed that it is, the other that it is not, and being unable to resolve the matter, each decided to write to the Pope for a definitive answer. After doing so they met again to share their results and were astonished to discover that the Pope had agreed with each of them. "How did you pose the question?" asked the first. The other replied, "I asked if it is permissible to smoke while praying. His Holiness said that it is not, since praying is a very serious business. And how did you phrase the question?" The first replied, "I asked if it is permissible to pray while smoking, and His Holiness said that it is, since it is always appropriate to pray."

The point, of course, is that the form in which a question is asked will control the kind of answer one gets, and that every question, therefore, has a fact or knowledge bias embedded in it. It is precisely this point that I meant to call to your attention in referring earlier to Mr. Macchiarola's incentives for reading scores. The question "How do we improve reading scores?" is not the same question as "How do we improve reading?" Moreover, the question "How do we improve reading?" is not the same question as "How do we improve language competence?"—which, as you gather by now, I regard as a more productive question than either of the other two. But here it is more to the point to say that whichever question one chooses to ask, the choice will control where and how we will look for the answers. A question is a structure for thought. Language education, therefore, must include the most serious exploration of the structure of questions—their assumptions, limitations, levels of abstraction, and the sources of authority to which they appeal. Without this knowledge our students can barely be said to know anything.

The second concept, referred to earlier, is that, although there is essential general knowledge to be learned about questions, each subject in a school curriculum has its own particular rules about questions. As I have implied, the questions that are appropriate in history differ in their form and meaning from those that are appropriate in biology, or mathematics, or literature. The reason for this is that each subject has a unique vocabulary and its own assumptions about what constitutes knowledge. Surely the "facts" of mathematics are not anything like what is meant by the "facts" of history. A biological "truth" is something quite different from "truth" in a literary work. A "correct" answer in physics is different from a "correct" answer in economics. Thus, through an exploration of how questions are asked in a subject, teachers of all subjects may lead their students to a careful consideration of the language that comprises their discipline. That is to say, any understanding of how a question may be asked in a subject presupposes an understanding of the unique language of that subject. And an understanding of a subject's language necessarily includes the study of the role of metaphor.

Unless I am sorely mistaken, metaphor is at present rarely approached in schools except by English teachers during lessons in poetry. This strikes me as an absurdity, since I do not see how it is possible for a subject to be understood in the absence of any insight into the metaphors on which it is constructed. There is no better example of this than the subject of education itself, for every philosophy, every proposal, every improvement one hears about is rooted in some metaphorical conception of the human mind, of knowledge, of the process of learning, and of the institution of school. In a fundamental sense, all arguments about how education ought to be conducted are arguments about the validity of competing metaphors. If you believe that the mind is like a dark cavern, you will suggest activities that are quite different from those suggested by people who believe the mind is like a muscle or an empty vessel. Do you believe that human beings learn the way rats learn? Or do you conceptualize the mind as a kind of computer? Or a garden? Or a lump of clay? Embedded in every test, every textbook, every teaching strategy, is a metaphor of the mind—some notion of what it is most nearly like. Similarly, arguments about the roles of teachers, students, and administrators originate in different metaphors of school. Some think of school as a prison; others, a hospital; still others, a military organization, or an extension of the home. How school is conceptualized will, in turn, control our metaphors of students. What are students? Are they patients to be cared for? Troops to be disciplined? Sons and daughters to be nurtured? Inmates to be punished? Resources to be cultivated? Personnel to be trained? It is right here, on this issue, that the arguments begin. One would think that adversaries in a dispute about education would try to make their metaphors explicit and visible, let us say, as scientists are apt to do. But usually they do not, which is one reason why such disputes tend to remain murky. To borrow a metaphor from linguistics, the deep structure of the argument usually remains hidden.

I do not mean to say that there is a "correct" metaphor of the mind or of learning. Neither do I say that a well-thought-out philosophy of education confines itself to a single one. I am saying that a conversation about education cannot extend beyond two or three sentences before a metaphor is invoked which provides structure, authority, or explanation for a certain belief. Or sometimes confuses the issue entirely. As I have implied, modern writers on education have not, in my opinion, been sufficiently aware of the extent to which their metaphors have controlled their thinking. This is in contrast to such venerable educationists as Plato, Cicero, Comenius, Locke, and Rousseau, who never failed to make their metaphors explicit. "Plants are improved by cultivation," Rousseau wrote in *Emile,* "and man by education." And his entire philosophy is made to rest upon this comparison of plants and children. Even in such ancient texts as the Mishnah, we find that there are four kinds of students: the sponge, the funnel, the strainer, and the sieve. It will surprise you to know which one is preferred. The sponge, we are told, absorbs all; the funnel receives at one end and spills out at the other; the strainer lets the wine drain through it and retains the dregs; but the sieve, that is the best, for it lets out the flour dust and retains the fine flour. The difference in education philosophy between Rousseau and the compilers of the Mishnah is precisely reflected in the difference between a wild plant and a sieve.

Again, I hope it is clear that at this point I am not arguing in favor of one metaphor as against another in education. I am merely pointing to the obvious fact that all disciplines in a curriculum, including education itself, are based on powerful metaphors which give direction and organization to the way we will do our thinking. In history, economics, physics, biology, or linguistics, metaphors, like questions, are organs of perception. Through our metaphors, we see the world as one thing or another. Is light a wave or a particle? Are molecules like billiard balls or force fields? Is language like a tree, or a river, or the ever-shifting wind? Is history unfolding according to some instructions of nature or divine plan? Are our genes like information codes? Is a literary work like a blueprint or a mystery to be solved? It is questions like these that preoccupy scholars in every field, because they are "basic" questions—which is to say, you cannot understand what a subject is about without some understanding of the metaphors which are its foundation. Do we want a "basic" education for our youth? Then we must explore with them that which is basic in a subject: its metaphors, as well as its questions.

To this must be added all of the issues involved in what may be called definition. There is no more depressing symptom of a "nonbasic" education than to hear a student ask for "the" definition of a term, since the question so often implies a lack of understanding of what a definition is and where definitions come from. Definitions, like questions and metaphors, are instruments for thinking. Their authority rests entirely on their usefulness, not their correctness. We use definitions in order to delineate problems we wish to investigate, or to further interests we wish to promote. In other words, we invent definitions and discard them as suits our purposes. And yet, one gets the impression that students (and not a few teachers) believe that God has provided us with definitions from which we depart at the risk of losing our immortal souls. This is the belief that I have elsewhere called "definition tyranny," which may be defined (by me,

not God) as the process of accepting without criticism someone else's definition of a word or a problem or a situation.
I can think of no better method of freeing students from this
obstruction of the mind than to provide them with alternative definitions of every concept and term with which they
must deal in a subject. Whether it be "molecule," "fact,"
"law," "art," "wealth," "gene," or whatever, it is essential
that students understand that definitions are hypotheses, and
that embedded in them is a particular philosophical, sociological, or epistemological point of view. One of the more
interesting examples of this idea is found, once again, in the
field of education. I refer to the meaning of the word "basic,"
as in "back to the basics." I would particularly like to call
to your attention that the meaning given to this word by
some educators is not its "real" meaning. The word "basic,"
like any other word, has no "real" meaning. It has been
assigned certain meanings in order to further an education
philosophy which is thought to be both sensible and effective.
The "basic" educators are entirely justified in doing this, but
neither you nor I are under any obligation to accept their
definition of what is "basic."

From my point of view, obviously, explorations of question-asking, metaphor, and definition are "basic"; nothing
that students are given to study can be properly considered
unless they know about the assumptions and structure of
questions, the controlling power of metaphor, and the origins
and motivations of definitions. I assume that Admiral Rickover, for example, does not regard these matters as "basic,"
which it is his privilege to do. But it is my privilege to prevent
him from preempting the word. I will use "basic" as I
choose, not as he chooses, and it is my intention to persuade
others that my definition is more useful than his. In short,
the definition of something is usually the starting point of a
dispute, not the settlement.

You now have some idea of my own definition of "language education," and of how central I believe it to be in the conservation and strengthening of intelligence. I have, of course, been discussing language in the context of the learning of subjects, from which I believe it to be inseparable. In the next chapter I will discuss language education from another point of view. But I have given language education in a knowledge context first priority here, because it is so uniformly ignored. What I am proposing is that in every subject —from history to biology to mathematics—students be taught, explicitly and systematically, the universe of discourse which comprises the subject. Each teacher would deal with the structure of questions, the process of definition, and the role of metaphor, as these matters are relevant to his or her particular subject. Here I mean, of course, not merely what are the questions, definitions, and metaphors of a subject, but *how* these are formed and how they have been formed in the past.

Students would also be taught how such terms as "right," "wrong," "truth," and "falsehood" are used in a subject, and what assumptions they are based upon. This is particularly important since words of this type cause far more trouble in students' attempts to understand a field of knowledge than do highly technical words. It is peculiar, I think, that of all the examinations I have ever seen, I have never come across one in which students were asked to say what is the basis of "correctness" or "falsehood" in a particular subject. Perhaps this is because teachers believe the issue to be too obvious for discussion or testing. If so, they are wrong. I have found that students at all levels rarely have thought about the meaning of such terms in relation to a subject they are studying. They simply do not know in what sense an historical fact is different from a biological fact. They do not even know how an historical fact is arrived at and by what procedures it may be shown to be false. Equally astonishing is that students, particularly those in elementary and secondary schools, rarely can express an intelligible sentence on the uses of the word "theory." Since most subjects studied in school consist largely of theories, it is difficult to imagine exactly what students are in fact studying when they do their history, biology, economics, physics, or whatever. It is obvious, then, that language education must include not only the serious study of what truth and falsehood mean in the context of a subject, but also what is meant by a fact, an inference, an assumption, a judgment, a generalization, and so on. In this way students will be learning both the language of a subject and the methods of inquiry in that subject, since inquiry consists of nothing else but the generation of questions, the invention of definitions and metaphors, the separation of facts from inferences, the forming of generalizations, and so on.

In addition, some attention must obviously be given to the style and tone of the language in a given subject. Each subject is a manner of speaking and writing. There is a rhetoric of knowledge, a characteristic way in which arguments, proofs, speculations, experiments, polemics, even humor, are expressed. One might even say that speaking or writing a subject is a performing art, and each subject requires a somewhat different kind of performance from every other. Historians, for example, do not speak or write history in the same way biologists speak or write biology. The differences have much to do with the kind of material they are dealing with, the degree of precision their generalizations permit, the type of facts they marshal, the traditions of their subject, the type of training they receive, and the purposes for which they are making their inquiries. The rhetoric of knowledge is not an easy matter to go into, but it is worth remembering that some scholars—one thinks of Veblen in sociology, Freud in psychology, Galbraith in economics—have exerted influence as much through their manner as their matter. The point is that knowledge is a form of literature, and the various styles of knowledge ought to be studied and discussed. I will grant that the language found in typical school textbooks tends to obscure this entire area. Textbook language is apt to be the same from subject to subject, and creates the impression that systematic knowledge is always expressed in a dull and uninspired monotone. I have found that, typically, the recipes found on the back of cereal boxes are written with more style and conviction than is a textbook description of the causes of the Civil War. Of the language of grammar books, I will not even speak, for to borrow from Shakespeare, it is unfit for a Christian ear to endure. But the problem is not insurmountable. Teachers who are willing to take the time can find materials which convey ideas in a form characteristic of their particular discipline.

As our students learn about the rhetoric of a subject, as they learn about the meaning of facts and assumptions in a subject, as they learn about the presuppositions of truth and falsehood, as they learn about how definitions, metaphors, and questions are formed, they would, of course, be learning how to read, write, speak, and listen to the subject. As Wendell Johnson once remarked, you cannot write writing. In the sense he meant it, neither can you read reading or speak speaking. You must write about something, just as you must read and speak about something. The "something" is often some aspect of human knowledge which has been given systematic expression in a particular kind of language. Thus all reading, in truth, is reading in a content area. To read the phrase "the law of diminishing returns" or "the law of supply and demand" requires that you know how the word "law" is used in economics, for it does not mean what it does in the phrase "the law of inertia" (physics) or "Grimm's law" (linguistics) or "the law of the land" (political science) or "the law of survival of the fittest" (biology). To the question, "What does 'law' mean?" the answer must always be, "In what context?"

Perhaps you will now understand more fully my earlier remarks about reading tests. A reading test of the sort usually given in school does not test reading any more than a context-free vocabulary exam tests one's understanding of how words are used. A reading test measures one's ability to read reading tests, and reading tests are in themselves a very peculiar sort of situation. The world of reading tests is somewhat akin to the world of crossword puzzles or Scrabble or the game of twenty questions. Some people play these games well, and all praise is due them for their skill. But if we ask, What aspect of the world do they comprehend in doing these games well? the answer is, Only the world within the games themselves.

To put it simply, the question, "How well does one read?" is a bad question, because it is essentially unanswerable. A more proper question is "How well does one read poetry, or history, or science, or religion?" No one I have ever known is so brilliant as to have learned the languages of all fields of knowledge equally well. Most of us do not learn some of them at all. No one is a "good reader," period. There are those, for example, who read the physical sciences well, but not history, and those who read political science well, but not poetry. Each discipline requires of the reader a particular set of abilities, store of knowledge, and frame of mind, so that there must always be great variability in our capacities to read, write, or speak in different subjects. I assume, for instance, that Admiral Rickover reads mathematics and engineering brilliantly. I should very much like to test his ability to read poetry or religion. I suspect he would fall below the "national norm" (whatever that means) on such a test. I have evidence from his writing that he is not at all skillful in the subject of education. He appears to me unaware of his own metaphors for teachers and students and the nature of mind; he confuses facts with inferences; he reifies definitions; he seems oblivious to the biases of his questions. In his limitations Admiral Rickover is no better or worse than most of us; in fact, probably better, since his command of the language of science is so rich and thorough that he has been able to achieve a just fame for his scientific work. Most of us do not learn to read or speak any subject half as well. Admiral Rickover has become a burden only because he has assumed that he can read and write education as well as he does engineering.

From what I have been saying about the teaching of language in a knowledge context, you may assume that I believe the following:

1. The improvement of language behavior requires increased knowledge of various aspects of human experience. The more you know about a subject, the better you can listen to it, and read, write, and speak it.

2. Knowledge of a subject means knowledge of the language of that subject, which includes not only what its words mean but, far more important, *how* its words mean. As one learns the language of a subject, one is also learning what the subject is. It cannot be said often enough that what we call a subject consists mostly, if not entirely, of its language. If you eliminate all the words of a subject, you have eliminated the subject. Biology is not plants and animals. It is language about plants and animals. History is not events. It is language describing and interpreting events. Astronomy is not planets and stars. It is a way of talking about planets and stars. Therefore, there are two levels of knowing a subject. There is the student who knows what the definition of a noun or a gene or a molecule is; then there is the student who shares that knowledge but who also knows how the definition was arrived at. There is the student who can answer a question; then there is the student who also knows what are the biases

of the question. There is the student who can give you the facts; then there is the student who also knows what is meant by a fact. I am maintaining that, in all cases, it is the latter who has a "basic" education; the former, a frivolous one.

3. I maintain further that such a "basic" education can begin in the earliest grades, and that it is not necessary for even a fourth grader to be burdened by such obstructions of the mind as definition tyranny, reification, superficiality, and total unawareness of what a subject is. The concepts to be studied in learning the language of knowledge may be presented in different ways and at variable levels of complexity; learning the language of knowledge is not beyond the range of elementary-school children. Moreover, since there is no such thing as complete knowledge of a subject, one is always working to improve one's reading, writing, etc., of a subject. As Thomas Henry Huxley said, "If a little knowledge is a dangerous thing, is there anyone who knows so much as to be out of danger?" The notion that reading and writing instruction, for example, may cease in the tenth or eleventh grade is nonsense. The fourth grader and the tenth grader are faced with the same sort of problem— learning about the uses of language in different subjects. That the latter may know more about it than the former does not imply that his instruction can end. The problems of learning to read or write are inexhaustible. Anyone who has worked with graduate students can tell you that they require continuous instruction in reading and writing their subject.

4. It is to be understood that the evaluation of a student's speaking or writing behavior must focus on whether or not he or she *makes sense,* on whether or not a student

knows what is being asserted and can respond to it in appropriate ways. But this does not mean that grammatical or rhetorical error is irrelevant in evaluating students. As I have said, each subject is a manner of speaking. An historian is not likely to say "Bullshit!" when he disagrees with another historian. That is the language of another universe of discourse. The difference between "Bullshit!" and "I disagree" is not solely a matter of propriety. It is a difference in outlook and usually reflects differences, not in social class, but in understanding of the kind of situation history or any other subject is. The same may be said of writing that is filled with mechanical and grammatical error, as compared with writing that conforms to the rules of standard edited English. Surely, we do not want to say that there is a necessary correlation between mechanical and editorial accuracy and intellectual substance. There are many books that are mechanically faultless but which contain untrue, unclear, or even nonsensical ideas. Carefully edited writing tells us, not that the writer speaks truly, but that he or she grasps, in some detail, the manner in which knowledge is usually expressed. The most devastating argument against a paper that is marred by grammatical and rhetorical error is that the writer does not understand the subject.

Thus, the quality of students' learning is to be judged by both their manner and their matter. And it is precisely through one's learning about the total context in which the language of a subject is expressed that personality may be altered. If one learns how to speak history or mathematics or literary criticism, one becomes, by definition, a different person. The point to be stressed is that a subject is a situation in which and through which people conduct themselves, largely in language. You cannot learn a new form of conduct without changing yourself.

5. I want, finally, to point out that the meaning I have given here to "language education" represents it as a form of meta-education. That is, one learns a subject and, at the same time, learns what the subject is made of. One learns to talk the subject, but also learns to talk about the talk; one learns subjects as human situations whose language is at all times problematic. If it be said that such learning will prevent students from assimilating the facts of a subject, my reply is that this is the only way by which the facts can truly be assimilated. For it is not education to teach students to repeat sentences they do not understand so that they may pass examinations. That is the way of the computer. I prefer the student to be a programmer.

9

Language Education in a Social Context

Role-playing, in the nontrivial meaning of the phrase, is a process of assuming the style, the outlook, the attitudes, and therefore in essence the language of someone we are not but whom we aspire to be. There is nothing phony about role-playing. It is the principal means by which we may refine and extend our intelligence. Through role-playing we may also shrivel our intelligence, everything depending on whom we have chosen to emulate. Role-playing, therefore, is always serious business in the context of education.

In the last chapter, I argued that by learning to talk, read, write, and listen the way learned people do, our youth may be shown an entrance to the world of systematic knowledge. People are not born as biologists or historians or literary critics. We learn how to do what they do by acting the way they do. When our act reaches a certain level of competence —when we can comfortably speak in their voice—then we have become what they are. The aim of language education in a knowledge context is to initiate the process of role transformation.

In the present information environment, this is an exceedingly important objective. As I have contended, the media curriculum promotes a persistent intellectual passivity, especially among our youth, and we cannot overcome its bias by fostering a similar kind of knowledge consumerism in the schools. By placing the language of the learned at the center of the school curriculum, we may help our young to go beyond ventriloquizing the content of the subjects they study and to achieve some insight into the structure of knowledge; in particular, into the structure of "knowledging." If the phrase "learning how to learn" means anything, it means learning how language gives shape and texture to knowledge, how language is deployed to make inquiries, how language controls our perceptions. "The result of the educative process," John Dewey wrote, "is the capacity for further education." Through familiarity with the means by which knowledge is codified, students may take the first steps toward such a result, even in the early grades.

But there is much more to life and, indeed, language than knowing how to act as a learned person does. Of all the sentences we utter, and listen to, in a lifetime only a small percentage will have very much to do with organized knowledge. Talking (and I should say, listening as well) is a performing art. Nothing marks the educated person more surely than individuality, originality, and variety in everyday language performances, such performances having an unlimited and continuous run. Thus, language education in a social context is just as important as language education in a knowledge context. However, in approaching the subject of the social uses of language—language as an instrument of everyday communication—we find ourselves in the midst of controversy. The controversy centers on what may be called "the politics of language," and has everything to do with role-playing.

In a simpler time, it was assumed that the language children brought with them to school was, at least in some of its details, defective. Part of the task of language education was to correct these deficiencies. Typically, it was held that children used grammar crudely, pronounced words sloppily, and had a woefully limited social vocabulary. It was the English teacher's job to loosen children from their incorrect language habits and to introduce them to the world of "correct English." This they tried valiantly to do but with generally poor results. One of the more formidable obstacles they faced was that they were—to use some modern jargon—unattractive role models. Very few students wanted to be like their English teachers and aggressively declined to talk like them. Among other things, their teachers were frequently precious, imperious, and even openly contemptuous of their students' backgrounds and linguistic deficiencies. The psychology of the situation was bad. But so was, so to speak, the epistemology. Many teachers were unclear and even ignorant about the sources of their knowledge and authority. They were not always able to explain, for example, why one form of usage was to be preferred over another, and time and again they had to fall back on an almost mystical conception of "correctness." Some expressions, it seems, were correct and some expressions were not. From the students' point of view, there was often no way to figure out which was which, except through what may be called "reverse English." I recall, when I was in grade school, passing several usage and grammar tests by identifying the form most comfortable to me, and then choosing the other one. For children from the Brooklyn working class, this was as good a way as any to get through English.

But in spite of the intellectual and psychological difficulties they faced, English teachers were, in more settled times, steadfast in their commitment to "correct English" and were widely regarded as guardians of the language. Though their students did not always know what correct English was, English teachers did, or so they thought, and it is part of our folklore that when one is in the presence of an English teacher, one makes a special effort to speak with care.

Much of what I have been describing seems to have changed within the past fifteen years. In particular the commitment of the schools to correct English has been undercut by two developments. The first has come from the field of linguistics. Linguists have been able to show that there isn't anything decisively more logical about correct English than incorrect English, that incorrect English is in some cases more historically justifiable than correct English, and that our notions about usage have more to do with our prejudices against people than anything else. It is not the "ain'ts" and "deeses and dems" that are objectionable to us as much as the people who use them. In speaking of correct and incorrect English, the linguists taught us, we were in fact speaking of correct and incorrect people. Thus, the linguists recast the entire matter of language into social and political terms. From this perspective, the teaching of correct English was revealed as an act of elitism, an exercise in the provinciality of a particular social class.

My Brooklyn speech, as it turned out, was as good as any other. In taking grammar and usage tests, I should not have needed to resort to reverse English. I would have been justified in selecting as "correct" those forms which were comfortable to me and my neighbors, who were, after all, just as good as any other people. This point of view has received support from the inevitable discovery that "black English" (which even in *my* neighborhood was thought to be primitive) is not a thoughtless corruption of some finer dialect but is itself a fully developed, coherent grammatical system. This discovery confirmed the assumption that dialects of every possible variety are equally complex and rich and that therefore no dialect could be regarded as inferior to any other.

The second development which undercut the rationale for the teaching of correct English occurred in the sociology of education. While the linguists were discovering that the basis of correct English had more to do with social class than with either logic or history, education critics discovered that all education was propaganda: Its aim was to effect changes in people. One would have thought this discovery too obvious to mention but from it a large and forceful criticism emerged, the central point of which is that schools try to merchandise the values and social habits of the middle class, including its preferred language. Thus, education was represented as oppressive to the poor and the lower classes, who are subjected, against their will, to the biases of a culture which despises them.

Out of this criticism, as well as from discoveries in linguistics, came the controversial manifesto of the National Council of Teachers of English in which it was proclaimed that students have "a right to their own language."[1] This meant that while Standard English (what used to be called correct English) had its special uses, in no sense was it to be regarded as generally superior to any other form of English. The language that students brought with them to school was to be accorded the same respect and possibly attention as the teacher would give to his or her own dialect. Oddly, the National Council of Teachers of English has also issued a proclamation of sorts urging teachers to expunge from their students' language any tendencies toward sexism. In other words, the student is granted the right to say "I ain't got none" but not the right to say "chairman."

The present situation, in short, is confused. It is no longer clear what English teachers ought to be doing in regard to language as an instrument of social discourse. Although it would be too much to say that most English teachers have abandoned teaching correct English, those who continue to do so must speak with much less authority than once they did. This is as it should be. We cannot go back to that simpler time before linguists and sociologists began examining what is meant, and what is implied, by "correct English." But it does not follow from this that language education in a social context must end or that the concept of good English must end with it. There is, I believe, an argument against the present tendencies which is consistent with a thermostatic view of education and, therefore, with its conserving function; that is to say, we *can* go back again although with a clearer idea of exactly what we are doing.

The first point to be made in developing this argument is to grant that concepts of good language do have a political bias. In putting forward as desirable the speech or writing of a particular class of people, one is asserting that such people are preferable, at least in some ways, to those who speak or write differently. So, if we are to teach *any* concept of good English, we are being elitist, which is a political position. But I can see no objection to this and do not understand why educators flee from its implications. All good education is elitist in that it says to a student, "You are not adequate as you are. There are better people than you. And you will be taught how they think, how they write, how they talk, and what they know." I find it hard to imagine what the alternative would be. Is it possible that a nonelitist education would say, "You are fine just as you are. What you know, whom you know, and what you value are not in need of improvement"?

If this were so, one would hardly require an education. To teach anything is to assert that one's student is inadequate. By its nature, teaching is an elitist activity, for elitism implies a hierarchy of values, as does teaching.

There was a time, of course, when none of this would have had to be said. It was taken for granted that one's education would put forward "role models" who were in some sense better than the student, or even the student's parents. But today the concept of "better than" has rapidly eroded, partly because of the nonhierarchical structure of media. An information environment which gives everyone access, simultaneously, to the same information has a strong egalitarian bias. It alters the politics of knowledge, creating the impression that there are no important differences among people; that so far as knowledge is concerned we are a classless society. Moreover, the attention-centered, market-oriented content of the media enhances the view that "better than" is an outdated, even ignoble idea. It is true, to be sure, that the media do promote the idea of self-improvement, but always, as noted earlier, against a standard of supreme technological expertise: People who use Scope or Comet are better than you are. But in most other matters the content, as well as the structure, of the media curriculum tends to mock hierarchies and teaches that any distinctions that might be made in taste, manners, style, language, or states of learning are invidious and pretentious. The culture heroes of the media—from John Travolta to Rocky to Fonzie to Laverne and Shirley— serve to celebrate the style, the achievements, the authenticity, of the common man, thus promoting an attitude that Bertrand Russell once called "democratic envy." In warning against this, Russell reminded us of the occasion when the ancient Ephesians banished Hermodorus from their land because he was a better man than the rest of them. "We will have none who is best among us," they said. "If there be such, let him be so elsewhere and among others." This form of blindness is one of the principal dangers of an aggressive egalitarianism, for it flattens out hierarchical distinctions and thereby banishes models of excellence. In a sense it makes education pointless.

What it comes down to is this: The media curriculum is, by its nature, nonelitist. It is the modern-day equivalent of the Ephesians, and tends to make invisible all role models that call into question the validity of folk-wisdom, folk-style, and folk-language. What I have said is hard for me to imagine turns out to be one of the principal teachings of the media curriculum, namely: "Except for your unaccountable ignorance of how the products of technology may help you to achieve happiness, you are fine just as you are. How you speak, what you value, and what you know require no improvement, for there is no other level of culture that is better than yours."

To which André Gide has offered the best reply I know. "The only real education," he said, "comes from what goes counter to you." In other words, it is precisely from the fact that our culture is suffused with the bias of nonelitism that our schools may find the warrant to be elitist. I use the word "elitist" here (as I have been using it) to mean putting forward a conception of behavior and thought, and in particular language, that is deemed "better than" what students usually feel most comfortable with. In our present situation, no school should exist without clear images of "better than"— in taste, in manners, in language. In the absence of such images, the school becomes essentially indistinguishable from the culture and therefore useless to it. In particular the school must have a standard of good language that goes counter to what the students practice and which transcends the bias of popular culture.

But in saying this I am not implying that a standard of good English must be maintained just so it may stand in opposition to prevailing practice. There are in fact very good reasons why some forms of English, and one in particular, may be regarded as better than others. The first is that what is called Standard English is the dialect in which most published writing occurs. As long as students have an inadequate knowledge of this dialect, they will be limited in what they can understand when reading and will, of course, be restricted in what they can write. Second, because Standard English is the dialect in which most of our literature is and has been encoded, it has a far wider range of expressiveness than any other form of English, and contains the fullest living account of the history and psychology of English-speaking people. By this I mean it has been used, in spoken and written form, by people of widely different time, place, social class, and experience to express every conceivable state of mind. There are very few ideas, feelings, or attitudes that might occur to an English-speaking person that cannot find adequate expression in Standard English. Its resources have been mined and developed by our most intelligent people and therefore there is a precision and richness to it that cannot be approached by any social, regional, or ethnic dialect.

Moreover, Standard English has embedded in it what we generally mean by taste in and refinement of expression. It has been some considerable time since the subject of taste has been discussed among either educationists or linguists. The subject is, in fact, irrelevant if one believes that intelligibility (or, as it is sometimes called, communication) is the only purpose of language. In that case, "Bullshit" and "I disagree," "I ain't got none" and "I don't have any," and "Chairman" and "Chairperson," are synonymous expressions. But this is patently false. There are no entirely synonymous expressions in language, for every word, phrase, and sentence carries with it an attitude. The challenge of an English sentence only begins with the problem of simple intelligibility. A sentence is also and always a statement of one's relationship to a listener, to a subject, to a tradition of manners, to an aesthetic standard. Language, in short, is a means of expressing in compact form many things, including one's level of refinement. Unless our schools abandon any attempt to convey what such words as style, elegance, and taste mean, Standard English must be the form which serves as a model of excellence and aspiration.

I am here talking mainly about the vocabulary and syntax of Standard English. In the matter of pronunciation, it would be somewhat more difficult to justify what I have been saying. But it is not accents I am talking about but access, access to the words, style, taste, and meanings of the most thoroughly literate of our population, now and in the past. Of course, I must hasten to say that nothing could be more ruinous than conveying to the young the idea that the user of Standard English is guaranteed access to truth or wisdom or even plain sense. Falsehood, stupidity, and nonsense are expressed in all dialects, perhaps in an equal distribution. But Standard English is the form in which the best that has been thought, said, and written in our language has been codified. It is the dialect not merely of the middle class or the power elite. It is the dialect of the "educated," whatever their class or influence, and the school is surely permitted to hold to a definition of what an educated person is. The media curriculum certainly does. While the students may be granted the right to their language, the school, in turn, must be granted the right to promote what it regards as the instrument of civilized discourse.

The question, then, is how might this be done? The first problem to solve is an empirical one of sorts. English teachers must know what Standard English is so that they can teach it. This is not as easy a problem as Edwin Newman and John Simon suppose. Standard English is by no means fixed, and there are no unassailable authorities to whom we can turn. As the linguists have shown, neither logic nor history is necessarily a reliable guide in the matter. And the question of who is and who is not an "educated" person is fraught with complexities. Moreover, English teachers themselves are not always well equipped to make sound generalizations about Standard English. On the one hand, there is Miss Fiddich, the legendary stereotype of an English teacher, whose conception of Standard English has a distinct leaning toward the eighteenth century. I happen to be partial to the language of that century myself but I am more than willing to acknowledge that the speech and writing of present-day educated people have undergone changes since then. Miss

Fiddich must acknowledge this, as well. Otherwise, she will impose on the young linguistic distinctions that are false to fact. The trouble with Miss Fiddich is that she has memorized too well the rules of the grammar text she uses, and has not listened well enough to the language of living literate people, including Edwin Newman and John Simon. But Miss Fiddich is not our most serious problem. Sad to say (for she has much to recommend her in our present situation), the Miss Fiddiches of the world are an irreversibly endangered species. Within a decade they will be gone. We have more to concern us on the other side of the picture. I refer to the younger, more culturally integrated, and ingratiating English teachers who are themselves products of the media curriculum. Their speech is barely distinguishable from that of their students, and they are often incapable of making accurate distinctions between educated and uneducated speech. Moreover, their writing is by no means entirely literate, and it is hard to see how they might exert a positive influence on the language knowledge and habits of their students.

The way out of this dilemma is twofold—through observation and imitation. Let us take observation first. In this context, it means that students should be encouraged by teachers of all states of learning to be active discoverers of what Standard English is. This does not necessarily mean the use of what are called "discovery methods" (although it does not exclude it). But it does mean that students must learn to listen to different patterns of speech and writing (for you can *listen* to writing) and to listen with sufficient concentration to distinguish between one form and another. It is next to useless, as all experience has shown, to provide students with rules to memorize or to ask them to receive passively statements about linguistic distinctions which they are not prepared to hear.

What is required are exercises and problems from which

students can verify to their own satisfaction any generalizations that might be made about Standard English, including
the differences between speech and writing. In fact, the greatest triumph of a teacher, in this matter, is to be refuted by
a student. A student who has not heard a distinction that the
teacher claims exists, or has heard one that the teacher is
unaware of, does not require, for all practical purposes, any
further instruction. In this connection the best use that can
be made of grammar and usage textbooks is to present their
information as hypotheses. Each statement in such a book
should be transformed into a question: Is it true that "who"
and "whom" are used by educated people in the manner that
the book claims? Is it true that no one begins a written
sentence with "and" or "but"? Is it true that sentences are
never ended with prepositions? Is it true that two negatives
make a positive?

In order to learn what Standard English is, students need
questions, not rules. They need to be made aware, not obedi-
ent. In saying this, I am not trying to revive some soppy
philosophy, from the reform movement of the sixties, about
the "autonomy of the child." In this context I am merely
talking about an effective learning strategy. The task of a
teacher—whether Miss Fiddich or any other kind—is to
generate, and to help students generate, questions which can
lead to awareness. From such questions students may not
only learn what good usage is and how it differs in specific
and realistic detail from their own speech and writing, but
they may also learn what is the basis for its preferred status.
This learning is particularly important in the present information environment. The media curriculum does not, at any
point, encourage the question, By what authority am I asked
to believe what I am seeing or hearing? It is a curriculum that
does not invite inquiry into itself. For this reason it is fundamentally authoritarian. An education that goes counter to
this bias would, of course, always consider two questions

in tandem—What is right? and Why is it alleged to be so?

One of the better ways to get at both these questions is through the process of translation. By presenting students with passages written in some familiar social or ethnic dialect and asking them to render the passages into Standard English, we may direct student attention to specific differences between the two forms of expression. And we may challenge students to locate the sources of their knowledge of Standard English. From tasks of this type, students may come to understand that "correctness" is not a static and mystical creation of textbooks but a dynamic performance by living people. Which leads us to imitation.

As the author of six textbooks designed to help students learn how to observe language, I can testify that such an approach does not work well unless it is accompanied by a desire to imitate the speech and writing of exemplary people. My own language education began in a serious way with my attempts to imitate the sentence structure, vocabulary, metaphors, and even cadence of two people: Red Barber and Franklin Delano Roosevelt. Red Barber, now justifiably enshrined (as they say) in baseball's Hall of Fame, was for many years the radio announcer for the Brooklyn Dodgers, now unjustifiably called the Los Angeles Dodgers. His descriptions of ball games struck me and many of my friends as so vivid and appealing, and at the same time so unusual, that imitating him actually became a summer's evening pastime. Each of several boys, in measured turns, would produce a fictional half-inning in the manner of Red Barber, subject of course to searing criticism from the others. I believe this sort of activity is called by educators "oral interpretation." It was from Red Barber that I first heard the words "ignominy" and "concomitant," neither of which I use very much today but from which I learned that such words can be used to describe real and important events, such as a Brooklyn–Cardinal game.

Of FDR I need only say that for the first thirteen years of my life he was the President of the United States, leading me to the erroneous conclusion that there either could not be or ought not be any other President of the United States. His "fireside chats" on radio brought a language style into our home that was both exotic and urgent, and to this day some of his phrases and sentences linger in my mind.

I know of no presidents or sportscasters today whose language can be expected to inspire an impulse to imitation. But teachers need not wait upon the accident of some unexpected source of motivation. There is no shortage of people, living or dead, whose language, spoken or written, may be put forward as an exemplary model. Although there is no way of predicting which students will be inspired by which people, the task of the teacher is to fill the classroom with enough models of excellence so that the chances of someone's finding someone are fairly good. My own list of writers would not fail to include (among the dead) Thomas Jefferson, John Adams, Thomas Paine, Abraham Lincoln, Mark Twain, Jane Austen, George Orwell, Bertrand Russell, Somerset Maugham, E. M. Forster, George Bernard Shaw, and Oscar Wilde. Each of them wrote clear and indisputably beautiful English sentences about important subjects. I can think of no more salutary exercise than to ask students, in the British manner of teaching writing, to imitate the sentences of each of them. Like Miss Fiddich, I am less sure of my ground in the matter of living people (as I am about excellent writers who would be suitable for young children to imitate) but the point is that every teacher ought to have gathered a list of contemporary writers whose sentences we would want to resonate in the minds of our students.

As for speech, the problem is the same—to locate people who use language with clarity, originality, and if possible, elegance; and to represent their speech as a standard to which students might aspire. Such people exist in great numbers and variety, and can be found among politicians, athletes, entertainers, and among other professionals who have continuous access to our ears. It must be remembered that children of all ages have a powerful impulse to imitate speech; and this impulse will be served whether teachers exploit it or not. I witnessed, not long ago, an incredible demonstration of this between two high school students who were approaching each other across a large field. When they came within hearing distance of each other, they started a sequence of greetings and salutations that turned out to be exact replications, in accent and vocabulary, of a routine by the comedian Steve Martin. Well, they could have done a lot worse than Steve Martin but surely this impulse to role-play through language can be used to go far beyond him. Occasionally there are even teachers—Miss Fiddich at her best is one—who understand that they have considerable potential as role models and who practice the art of speaking clearly, and with both style and variety. Needless to say, teachers who do this with an air of contempt or pomposity will defeat their purpose and offer no competition to Steve Martin. It must be stressed that students, especially in elementary school, do not usually resent a teacher who serves as a model of precise and original speech. It can become a "psychological issue" in the upper grades as the young become increasingly committed to their own level of culture and especially if the school does not offer a clear vision of an acceptable alternative.

The point is that whatever some liberal critics may think, our students do not require school to validate their natural way of speaking. Neither do they require school to grant them the right to use their own language. The home, the street, the playground, TV, movies, and radio disc jockeys will provide children with all the validation that is good for them and all the rights to their own language they will need. If the school is to be useful, it must not replicate the biases of the culture. It must provide a vision of something different and a concept of something better. That is what a school is for.

10
Media
Education

Education conceived along the lines of a thermostatic activity would inevitably have as one of its principal aims helping youth to step outside of and above their information environment so that they can see where they are located. This "stepping above" is what is meant, I believe, by having one's consciousness raised; in this case, about membership in the human race. Every proposal I have so far made —in language education, history education, science education, art education—has had something like that as its purpose. To see the ascent of humanity (or, for that matter, its descent) requires that you be positioned some distance away from the influences of your own times. If you are held captive in the midst of things, it is hard to know if humanity is going up or down, or moving at all. It is even hard to know if *you* are moving up or down.

Of all the subjects one might study in the hope of gaining a liberated perspective, none is more useful than what I shall call here "media ecology." At present no such subject exists in the schools except at the level of graduate education, which means, so far as I am concerned, that the schools need

to get busy, and at every level from elementary school
through college.

Media ecology is the study of information environments.
It is concerned to understand how technologies and techniques of communication control the form, quantity, speed,
distribution, and direction of information; and how, in turn,
such information configurations or biases affect people's perceptions, values, and attitudes. Thus, media ecology transcends several subjects of wider acceptance, including, for
example, psychology and sociology, since it assumes that the
psychology of people and their methods of social organization are, in large measure, a product of a culture's characteristic information patterns. As I have tried to say earlier in the
book, such information forms as the alphabet, the printed
word, and the television image are not mere instruments
which make things easier for us. They are environments—
like language itself, symbolic environments—within which
we discover, fashion, and express our humanity in particular
ways. When we talk of the psychology of a culture or its
sociology, we are talking about the effects of information
forms, at least to an extent that is often abysmally underestimated.

In the chapter "The Information Environment" I have
tried to explain this idea in some detail, particularly through
the examples I provided. To these examples I should like to
add another, taken from Lewis Mumford's *Technics and
Civilization.* In discussing the shaping power of new information forms, Mumford contends that the invention of both the
telescope and the microscope, taken together, had the effect
of completely undermining the conception of space common
to medieval man. He writes: "One invention increased the
scope of the macrocosm; the other revealed the microcosm.
Between them, the naive conceptions of space that the ordi-
nary man carried around were completely upset; one might
say that these two inventions, in terms of the new perspec-

tive, extended the vanishing point towards infinity and increased almost infinitely the plane of the foreground from which those lines had their point of origin."[1]

I bring forward this quotation for two reasons. First, it suggests how a technology which begins by giving us access to new facts about the world may end by creating new *ideas* about the world. Discovering the unseen world of remote stars and the secret presence of intimate microbes is not merely a matter of acquiring new sense data. Such a discovery leads to a reconceptualization of what there is to see, how things might be seen, and what there is to know. It may affect not only our conception of space, which is what Mumford is here discussing, but our conceptions of human relations and institutions. In extending the scope of our senses, a technology extends the scope of our imagination, a point well understood by the Catholic Church in Galileo's time. The Church knew, as Galileo perhaps did not, that his telescopic observations were not mere additions to knowledge of the cosmological world. They were in fact challenges to our theological world. If the earth moves in relation to the sun, then the position of man in relation to God must move as well. Galileo's telescope made God into a metaphor.[2]

To come closer to our own times: It is perhaps not fanciful to say that both the telescope and microscope provided the metaphysical perspective out of which was formed Freud's theory of the unconscious and his method of psychoanalysis. For in revealing spheres of influence which cannot be seen by the naked eye, these technologies intimate the existence of inner spheres of influence similarly hidden from view. The id becomes the microbes of the mind; psychoanalysis, the microscope. Although I would be hard put to "prove" this particular connection, the point I am making is that technology is always an idea disguised as a piece of machinery. To go beyond the machinery to the idea is the quest of media ecology.

The second reason I have used Mumford's quotation is that it was written forty-five years ago. Published in 1934, *Technics and Civilization* may be regarded as a fundamental text in media ecology, and is in any case the first comprehensive attempt to document the psychological and social changes brought about by technology. Since 1934 scores of historians, philosophers, sociologists, and anthropologists, among others, have allied themselves with Mumford's effort to catalogue and explain the effects of technology and technique. Among them are Harold Innis, David Riesman, Reuel Denney, Sigfried Giedion, Norbert Wiener, Edmund Carpenter, Eric Havelock, Walter Ong, Lynn White, Margaret Mead, Marshall McLuhan, Edward Hall, Joseph Weizenbaum, and Jacques Ellul. The subject which they invented, and which I have here merely given the name "media ecology," is complex, substantial, and provocative. When it is taught at the graduate level, the full richness of its interdisciplinary literature can be introduced, and students may undertake researches of genuine originality. But the subject may also be taught in the schools, and it is the purpose of this chapter to suggest how that might be done; in other words, how we might provide youth with an adequate media education.

It is best to begin by saying what media education is not. It is not the use of modern media, in or out of the classroom, to complement traditional studies. While there are some uses of TV, records, and films that can be justified—for example, to expose students to music they are not accustomed to hearing, or to plays they would have little opportunity to see —modern media should be brought into the classroom principally as specimens to analyze, not as aids. The Second Curriculum must study, evaluate, and criticize the First, not make alliances with it. The spectacle of education associations, for example the NEA, giving awards to such as Joan Cooney for her work in bringing *Sesame Street* to life is akin to the Railroad Workers of America commemorating the birthdays of the Wright Brothers. *Sesame Street* is television. Brilliant television, I might add. But what it teaches is what Burger King commercials teach. It teaches what television always teaches, and I refer you back to Chapter Three for what these teachings are. But as a further example of the futility of the schools' allying themselves with television, or other modern media, I offer *Watch Your Mouth,* a comedy series produced by Ellis B. Haizlip for WNET (an affiliate of the Public Broadcasting Service), under a grant awarded by the US Department of Health, Education, and Welfare. Its purpose is to "upgrade language and communication skills for teenagers." According to *Thirteen,* which is WNET's monthly guide, *Watch Your Mouth* uses "a situation drama/comedy format (Haizlip calls it 'ed com') to attract and hold the attention of its teenage target audience, who, studies indicate, consistently prefer dramas and family situation programs incorporating characters from their peer groups."

Aside from the fact that we are not told what the "teenage target audience" prefers dramas and family situations *to,* and aside from the fact that we do not require "studies" to know that children like television "sitcoms," we can tell what Mr. Haizlip has in mind here: *Welcome Back, Kotter.* "Our task," Mr. Haizlip says, "was to approach the series content both dramatically and academically. First our linguistic experts developed a lesson plan for each program in the series. Then our writers developed a story line for each half-hour episode. It then became the job of linguists to determine how the lesson could be woven into the drama. Sometimes the drama in itself became the lesson. We hope people understand that this is just another way of communicating."

I have seen *Watch Your Mouth,* accompanied by teenagers, and I can report that Mr. Haizlip knows what he is talking about. He is in fact too modest. The drama itself is not *sometimes* the lesson. It is *always* the lesson, for reasons

I have tried to indicate in Chapter Three. Notice, for example, that the lessons are woven into the drama, not the other way around. It is in the nature of television that this must be so. Moreover, I share with Mr. Haizlip the hope that people will understand that this is another way of communicating. However, I believe Mr. Haizlip does not quite understand his own sentence. By saying his "ed com" is *just* another way of communicating, he obviously means to imply that one way serves the same purpose as another. I am willing to stake everything on the belief that he is wrong, that an "ed com" cannot have both dramatic and academic content, that Mr. Haizlip does not know what academic content means, and that *Watch Your Mouth* would have been vastly improved by eliminating the "linguistic experts" and adding John Travolta to the cast.

The idea that Mr. Haizlip has sold to HEW is that TV entertainment and education can be made indistinguishable from one another. In one sense he is correct, since TV always teaches while it entertains. But it does not teach what he claims it teaches. It does not teach ideas or concepts or methods of analysis, and it cannot convey in an organized, or disorganized, way academic content. For academic content implies—is inseparable from—the form in which it is codified: abstract, digital, sequential symbolism. A statement about the meaning of a play may be academic content. The play cannot be. Which is why Plato banished the poets. The moving finger and the moving image are not, in any sense, equivalent ways of communicating. This is lesson number one in understanding media.

I have had powerful confirmation of this point from my own experience as a TV "teacher" on CBS's *Sunrise Semester*. From September 1976 to January 1977 I taught a "course" on the subject of communication—forty-eight half-hour programs. The course was seen in more than sixty cities across the country by approximately two million people, fifteen hundred of whom were moved to write me letters. Before saying what the content of these letters was, I should point out that *Sunrise Semester* is, to say the least, not a fast-paced, visually dynamic television program. It is nothing like *Watch Your Mouth.* It features what TV directors disdainfully call a "talking head," that is, a professor who is more or less immobile, viewed from no more than two perspectives. The cameras do not move, and there is a minimum of visual distraction from the ideational content of the professor's course. This is television used to replicate the lecture platform: all exposition and no drama. That is why *Sunrise Semester* is shown at six o'clock in the morning.

And yet, among the fifteen hundred letters I received, less than fifty had anything to do with academic content, and among those many merely requested that I repeat the name of a book or author I had mentioned, or spell the name of some concept I had discussed. (Easily the best letter about academic content came from a woman who advised me that she was having difficulty locating one of our texts, to which she referred as Erving Goffman's *Behavior in Pubic Places.* The title of the book is *Behavior in Public Places.*) The bulk of the letters addressed themselves to what I was wearing, what relative or actor I looked like, my need for a haircut, my mannerisms, my friendliness or aloofness, my moods, etc. I do not report this to deprecate my "fans," but to make the point that they *are* fans, or at least an audience witnessing TV performances. They are not "students," a fact which they well understood. Talking head or not, a moving image had come into their homes, and their response was as to a drama. But since there was no drama, their attention was on our relationship and on their feelings about that relationship, which is how fans are supposed to respond. These letter writers knew better than the officials at HEW what television is about and what is to be learned from it.

I have mentioned all of this because I feel it necessary to

labor the point that media education does not mean, as so many have suggested, the use of media. It means the investigation of media, the discovery of how our thought and behavior are controlled by our communications technology. Such investigations ought properly to begin with historical background, even in elementary school. A Gallup poll in 1978 revealed that of 1087 teenagers who were asked in what year Columbus discovered America, only fifty-one percent knew. The poll did not say what this statistic meant but we can assume that it confirms what we already know: Our youth have no head for historical facts, and probably very little interest in history; which makes history, as I have stressed, particularly relevant to their education. Accordingly, our students ought to be taught what ideographic writing is, who used it, and for what purposes. They ought to know where the alphabet comes from and something of its development. They ought to know about the beginnings of mathematics, and how the invention of the zero changed the way we think about numbers. They should be taught about illuminated manuscripts, the printing press, and the origins of newspapers and magazines. They ought to know about censorship and the arguments for and against freedom of expression. They ought to know where clocks, telescopes, microscopes, and computers come from. The names Morse, Bell, Edison, Marconi, DeForest, Zworykin, Pulitzer, Hearst, and Eisenstein ought to be familiar to them. In short, our students need to be provided with some sense of the historical development of communications technology.

As students move to higher grades, they may begin to consider, within an historical context, some important media ecological questions. I refer to such questions as: How does information differ in symbolic form? How are ideographs, for example, different from letters? How are images different from words? How are paintings different from photographs?

How is speech different from writing? How is mathematics different from language?

How do media differ in their physical forms? What difference does it make if a medium is durable but not portable as against a medium that is portable but not durable? How do messages differ in their speed of transmission, and what difference might this make? Why are some codes accessible to great numbers of people and some more or less secret? How is this difference likely to affect political ideas?

What media have helped us to "conquer" space? Or time? How have space and time "conquered" us? Which media stress the importance of which senses? What media stress individuality? What media stress communal experience?

The questions are almost inexhaustible. To list most of the important ones and to suggest their answers would require a book all by itself. Fortunately there exist many such books, and in the Notes section relating to this chapter I have listed several that teachers might use, including some textbooks.[3] The important points to keep in mind are that we are concerned here with the formal properties of information and how these properties affect psychological, social, and political life. To oversimplify more than is probably justified, we might say that (1) because of the symbolic forms in which information is encoded, different media have different *intellectual* and *emotional* biases; (2) because of the accessibility and speed of their information, different media have different *political* biases; (3) because of their physical form, different media have different *sensory* biases; (4) because of the conditions in which we attend to them, different media have different *social* biases; (5) because of their technical and economic structure, different media have different *content* biases.

Inquiries into these aspects of media and culture tend to be both abstract and historical, and probably should not be undertaken until junior high school. They can certainly be pursued in high school, and Marshall McLuhan himself has written an excellent text that may be used toward this end. But at all levels—although obviously with varying degrees of complexity—analyses of contemporary media should be undertaken vigorously. By this I mean that films, records, radio, and television should be brought into class as objects of study. As a general rule I would say that no TV set or film projector or record player should be turned on in the classroom unless the teacher intends to call attention to how the medium affects the audience. At all times, what we want to know is how a medium such as TV or radio structures our time, and how it creates a concept of time; how it affects our social relations; in what ways it stimulates our senses; how it treats "ideas"; how it conveys attitudes about authority, community, personal identity, etc.

The matter of content emphatically enters the picture here, and one hopes that teachers will be able to lead students in addressing questions concerning the psychological and sociological meaning of the content of the media. Students need to consider what movies and radio and TV programs are about at the content level, and what values they promote; that is to say, media education must include a serious treatment of popular culture (as it is called by those who favor it) or mass culture (as it is called by those who reject it). For this purpose, it is not always necessary to have a television set or radio or record player in the classroom. If there is one thing we can be sure our youth are familiar with, it is the content of the popular arts.

As you might guess, I believe the schools ought to take a less than benign view of this material since it would be important for the education of our youth that we promote standards of taste, as well as social values, that run counter to those promoted by modern media. I have, for example, already commented on the fact that the culture heroes of the media rarely include people of refinement and broad education. The sociological bias of the media needs no support from the schools. What it needs is criticism. But criticism must be based on understanding. For example, our students ought to know something about the origins of the folklore to which they are now continuously exposed. (Purists call the modern genres "fakelore.") Where, for example, does the TV western come from? Where did "cops and robbers" programs originate? Where do the themes on which so much advertising is based come from? What is the connection between folk heroes of the past and those of the present?

Our students also need to explore the social themes of electronic literature. What attitudes, for example, toward authority, freedom, civility, order, love, etc., are put forward as desirable by the content of popular songs, films, and TV programs? In this connection it is probably not necessary to make a distinction between what are called "programs" and what is called "advertising" in the popular arts. It seems obvious that on television, for example, commercials are merely time-compressed programs and that their themes and values are continuous with those of, say, *Happy Days* or *Welcome Back, Kotter.* The main difference between a "program" and a "commercial" is that the former is listed in the *TV Guide* and the latter is not. This fact suggests that our students need to know about the economic structure of media. Who, for example, determines what they will see and hear? Where does the money come from? What political interests are protected by the media?

There is so much to know about the forms, the themes, the economics, and the origins of the popular arts (or mass culture), and so much to be gained from knowing it that it would surely be necessary to provide several courses in the subject, and to have such courses sequenced; that is, extending from elementary school through college. (In this context I can think of no better text for use in either high school or college that Reuel Denney's *The Astonished Muse: Popular Culture in America.*)

But this is far from the end of it. One of the main differences between the terms "popular arts" and "mass culture" is that the former usually includes only those products of modern technology that in some sense may be thought of as literature or folklore. The term "mass culture" spreads a wider net, and is apt to include investigations of all modern technologies and widely employed techniques. Thus, in studying mass culture, one considers everything from fast-food restaurants to jet planes to computers to credit cards to IQ tests. The courses in media education (or media ecology) which I am proposing should certainly include discussions of the impact of these technologies and techniques. In fact, I can think of few curriculum innovations more useful than the schools' giving a special course called "The Technicalization of America."

As an example of what I have in mind—that is, of its necessity—I refer to an event I witnessed on television not long ago. The program was called *The Miss Universe Beauty Pageant.* Now, an analysis of the meaning of "beauty contests" could, all by itself, occupy weeks of constructive academic work, under the rubric of "mass culture studies." But here, I am especially concerned to note the uses of a computer in the proceedings. As each contestant came forward to reveal the quality of her body or mind (for each was asked questions about her life in an effort to determine her "poise"), the several judges rated her through the use of a computer. With legendary speed, a mother-computer then determined the average of all ratings, which was instantly posted on the television screen. Thus, Miss Holland, for example, was a 4.237 on how she looked in a bathing suit, and a 6.231 on poise. (The Master of Ceremonies, sounding very much like an English teacher I once knew, had announced that poise was to be determined not by what the contestant said but by how she said it, which, come to think of it, might well be the motto of all television.)

Aside from the fact that this kind of technicalization has obvious similarities to what we presently do in school, it raises these questions: What sort of people are we that value the quantification of poise and bathing-suit appearance? What is to be gained from such quantification, and what is to be lost? To what extent are the brilliance and ingenuity of the computer the real main event in those situations in which the computer is used? It occurred to me as I watched the numbers flashing on the screen that America does not have to prepare itself for the "metric system." We are already living what the British social historian Harry Hopkins calls "the metred life"—the effort to translate all experience into numbers. The computer not only has made this easier to do; I believe it intensifies the desire to do it. Perhaps it even creates the need to do it.

I obviously mean to suggest here that there is something very close to psychopathic about the intrusion of the computer in every conceivable aspect of human affairs. And I believe a similar accusation can be made against the use of many other techniques that are now part of our social lives. But far more important than one man's opinion is that the *question* of the value of technicalization needs to be part of our students' media education. It may be approached in a course called "The Technicalization of America," or it may be approached in a sequence of courses concerned with "mass culture." Whatever the formal structure, we might well begin by considering the "metred life" as it is lived in school. It is always best to begin at home and with something basic. What, for example, is a test? In what sense do tests *measure* things? What does "measurement" mean? What things can be measured and what things cannot? What does one have to know in order to measure another person?

Obviously I am not speaking against testing, or, for that matter, computers. I am speaking for students' having access to knowledge about the assumptions of various techniques that make up our culture. Courses in mass culture or the process of technicalization might include a consideration of the role of bureaucracy, of the meaning of efficiency, of the value of precision, of the function of quantification. Such courses might include as specimens for examination a wide variety of techniques and technologies—from beauty contests to jet planes to fast-food dispensaries. The purpose of these courses would be to show how a technique or technology always embodies an idea. McDonald's, in other words, may be a restaurant but it is also a technique. And as a technique, it is also a philosophy—a theory, if you will—about leisure, about time, about social relations, about efficiency, about the meaning of food. A beauty contest is a technique, reflecting an idea about women, about sex, about the measurement of measurements. And an IQ test is also, first and foremost, an idea—about the meaning of intelligence, about the forms of its expression, about the relation of intelligence to time. As the telescope and microscope altered our conceptions of space because they were ideas, so do the automobile and jet plane and credit cards, because they too are ideas.

To put it plainly, the general purpose of all media education—whether it concerns the history, the effects, or the values of media—is to help students see culture as forms of information that both reflect and create the prevailing way of life. And in this connection, what we call a "classroom" is also a technique which embodies a wide variety of ideas about learning. It is time we turned our attention to it, since everything I have proposed so far will take place there.

11
The Classroom

I should like to begin this discussion of the classroom with an apology to Mr. William O'Connor, wherever he is. Mr. O'Connor, who is unknown to me in a personal way, was once a member of the Boston School Committee, in which capacity he made the following remark: "We have no inferior education in our schools. What we have been getting is an inferior type of student."

At the time this statement was made (about 1968), I happened to be editing a book on the misuses of language, and I included his observation, among several others, as an example of semantic nonsense. It seemed to me at the time that the quality of an education had nothing whatever to do with the "quality" of a student. No matter what their abilities, students are entitled to an education that is suitable to them. If it is not, the problem is with the education, not the student. Mr. O'Connor's remark, I judged, was analogous to the defense of a clothing manufacturer who refuses to produce anything but large-sized pants. When business falls off, he explains his problem by saying, "Our pants are just fine. What we have been getting is too many little people."

Now, it is possible that Mr. O'Connor was indeed thinking along these lines, in which case I was not mistaken in my original judgment. But I wish to apologize to him anyway because there is a point of view from which his remark is perfectly sound. There are in fact a couple of senses in which we might say that school is good but some students aren't; and perhaps one or both of these is what Mr. O'Connor had in mind.

To come to the point: A classroom is a technique for the achievement of certain kinds of learnings. It is a workable technique provided that both the teacher and the student have the skills, and particularly the attitudes, that are fundamental to it. Among these, from the student's point of view, are tolerance for delayed gratification, a certain measure of respect for and fear of authority, and a willingness to accommodate one's individual desires to the interests of group cohesion and purpose. As I have previously argued, these attitudes cannot be easily taught in school because they are a necessary component of the teaching situation itself. The problem is not unlike trying to find out how to spell a word by looking it up in the dictionary. If you do not know how a word is spelled, it is hard to look it up. In the same way, little can be taught in school unless these attitudes are present. And if they are not, it is difficult to teach them.

Obviously, such attitudes must be learned during the six years before a child starts school; that is, in the home. This is the real meaning of the phrase "preschool education." If a child is not made ready for the classroom experience at home, he or she cannot usually benefit from any normal school program. But just as important, the school, in turn, is defenseless against such a child, who, typically, is a source of disorder in a situation that requires order as a precondition. I raise this issue here, and first, because there can be no education reform, at least as I have been proposing it, unless there is order in the classroom. Everyone seems to know this except some advanced education critics. Without the attitudes that lead to order, the classroom is an entirely impotent technique. Therefore, one possible translation of Mr. O'Connor's remark is, "We have a useful technique for educating youth but too many of them have not been provided at home with the attitudes necessary for the technique to work." There is nothing nonsensical about such an observation. In fact, it calls to mind several historical instances where some magnificent technology was conceived, only to remain undeveloped because the conditions for its creative use did not exist. The Aztecs, for example, invented the wheel but applied it only to children's toys since the terrain on which they lived made it useless for any other purpose. The Chinese invented the printing press centuries before Gutenberg. But saddled with a picture writing-system, with thousands of symbols, they were unable to use it as a medium of mass communication. In the same way, a classroom cannot be used for the purposes I have been proposing in this book unless the children who come to it are emotionally and intellectually prepared for its uses. A classroom, like a wheel or a printing press, *can* be a well-designed instrumentality but at the same time can be useless to those who are not ready for it. There are limits to its flexibility. To use my clothing analogy again: A manufacturer of pants—large, medium, *and* small—can do no business with a person who wears none.

There is still another way in which Mr. O'Connor's remark makes plain sense. I have been arguing throughout this book that the information environment in which we live does not give support to the attitudes that are fundamental to the classroom. The First Curriculum "unreadies" all youth for the structure of the Second, and thereby seriously endangers it. Mr. O'Connor's remark may also be translated to read: "We do not have an inferior education, if it were the nineteenth century. Our problem is that we have been getting students who are products of the twentieth century." But there is nothing nonsensical about this, either. The nineteenth century had much to recommend it, and we certainly may be permitted to allow it to exert an influence on the twentieth. It is precisely for this reason that the biases of the traditional classroom need to be maintained. The classroom *is* a nineteenth-century invention, and we ought to prize what it has to offer. It is, in fact, one of the few social organizations left to us in which sequence, community experience, social order, hierarchy, continuity, and deferred pleasure are important.

Thus, the problem of disorder in the classroom is largely created by two factors: a dissolving family structure out of which come youngsters who are "unfit" for the presuppositions of a classroom, and a radically altered information environment which undermines the foundations of school. The question, then, arises, What should be done about the increasing tendency toward disorder in the classroom?

Liberal reformers, such as Kenneth Keniston, have answers, of a sort. Keniston argues that economic reforms should be made so that the integrity and authority of the family can be restored. He believes that poverty is the main cause of family dissolution, and by improving the economic situation of families, we may kindle a sense of order and aspiration in the lives of children. Some of the reforms he suggests in his book *All Our Children* seem to me practical although they are very long range and offer no immediate response to the problem of disorder. Some utopians, such as Ivan Illich, have offered other solutions; for example, dissolving the schools altogether, or so completely restructuring the school environment that its traditional assumptions are rendered irrelevant. To paraphrase Karl Kraus's epigram about psychoanalysis, these proposals are the utopian disease of which they consider themselves the cure.

One of the best answers, from my point of view, comes

from Dr. Howard Hurwitz, who is neither a liberal reformer nor a utopian. It is a good solution, I believe, because it tries to respond to the needs not only of children who are unprepared for school by parental failure but of children of all backgrounds who are being made strangers to the assumptions of school.

Until his retirement Dr. Hurwitz was the principal of Long Island City High School in New York, where he became at once famous and infamous for suspending a disruptive student. Dr. Hurwitz, in his turn, was suspended by the board of education for being too quick on the suspension trigger, the board not exactly being slow itself. It should be noted that during the eleven years he was principal at Long Island City High School, the average number of suspensions each year was three, while in many New York City high schools the average runs close to one hundred. It must also be noted that during Dr. Hurwitz's tenure at Long Island City, there was not one instance of an assault on a teacher, and daily student attendance averaged better than ninety percent, which in the context of the New York City school scene represents a riot of devotion. All of the students at Dr. Hurwitz's school are, like youth everywhere, deeply influenced by the biases of the media, and many of them come from the kind of home background which does not prepare them well for school. Yet, he seems to have solved much better than most the problem of disorder.

Before giving the impression that Dr. Hurwitz should be canonized, I must say that I am more than a little familiar with his curriculum ideas, which he has widely advertised since his retirement, and many of them, in my opinion, are not worth the telling, at least not in a book of mine. But Dr. Hurwitz understands a few things of overriding importance that many educators of more expansive imagination do not.

The first is that educators must devote at least as much attention to the immediate consequences of disorder as to its abstract causes. One is sure that Dr. Hurwitz is as aware of the debilitating effects of poverty and disorganized home situations as anyone else. He may even understand the role of media in undermining the assumptions of school. But what he mostly understands is that whatever the causes of disorder and alienation, the consequences are severe and if not shackled result in making school impotent. Thus, at the risk of becoming a symbol of reaction, he ran what I believe is called "a tight ship." He holds to the belief, for example, that a child's right to an education is terminated at the point where the child interferes with the right of other children to have one. In other words, Dr. Hurwitz is a civil libertarian but of a type not always recognizable to the American Civil Liberties Union: He wants to protect the rights of the majority.

He also understands that disorder expands proportionately to the tolerance for it, and that children of all kinds of home backgrounds can learn, in varying degrees, to function in situations where there is no tolerance for it. He does not believe, by the way, that it is inevitably the children of the poor or only the children of the poor who are disorderly. But he knows that in spite of what the "revisionist" education historians may say, poor people still regard the schools as an avenue of social and economic advancement for their children, and do not object in the least to its being an orderly and structured experience. The hundreds of parents (many of whom are among the "poor and oppressed") who vigorously defended him after his suspension will testify to this.

What all this adds up to is the commonsense view that the school ought not to accommodate itself to disorder, or to the biases of other communication systems. The children of the poor are likely to continue to be with us. Some parents will fail to assume competent responsibility for the preschool education of their children. The media will increase the intensity of their fragmenting influence. These are facts educators must live with. But Dr. Hurwitz believes, nonetheless, that as a technique for learning the classroom can work if students are oriented toward its assumptions, not the other way around. Mr. William O'Connor, wherever he is, would probably agree. And so do I. The school is not an extension of the street, the movie theater, a rock concert, or a playground. And it is certainly not an extension of the psychiatric clinic. It is a special environment which requires the enforcement of certain traditional rules of controlled group interaction. The school may be the only remaining public situation in which such rules have any meaning at all, and it would be a grave mistake to change those rules because some children find them hard or cannot function within them at all. Children who cannot ought to be removed from the environment in the interests of those who can. This is an action Dr. Hurwitz was not loath to take, although it should be stressed that he did not need to do so often. Wholesale suspensions are a symptom of disorder, not a cure for it. And what makes Hurwitz's school noteworthy is the small number of suspensions that have been necessary. This is not the result of his having "good" students or "bad" students. It is the result of his creating an unambiguous, rigorous, and serious attitude —a nineteenth century attitude, if you will—toward what constitutes acceptable school behavior. In other words, Dr. Hurwitz's school turns out to be a place where children of all kinds of backgrounds—the fit and unfit—can function, or can learn to function. And where the biases of our information environment are emphatically opposed.

At this point, I should like to leave the particulars of Dr. Hurwitz's solution and, retaining their spirit, indicate some particulars of my own. I suspect you will think in reading them that I have turned my back on twentieth-century "liberalism," which would be entirely correct.

Let us start, for instance, with the idea of a dress code. I believe it to be a splendid rule from which the atmosphere in a school cannot fail to improve. What a dress code signifies is that school is a special place in which special kinds of behaviors are required. The way one dresses is always an indication of an attitude toward a situation. And the way one is *expected* to dress indicates what that attitude ought properly to be. You would not wear dungarees and a T-shirt which says "Feel Me" when attending a church wedding. If you did, it would be considered an outrage against the tone and meaning of the situation. The school has every right and reason, I believe, to expect the same sort of consideration.

Those who are inclined to think this is a superficial point are probably forgetting that symbols not only reflect our feelings but to some extent create them. One's kneeling in church, for example, reflects a sense of reverence but it also engenders reverence. Put an atheist or a cynic in church and have him kneel before an altar. He may be surprised to find certain feelings coming upon him that are not unlike those experienced by the devout. The effect of symbolic action on our minds should never be underestimated, for our behavior may lead to feeling as much as feeling may lead to behavior. As William James observed in his *Talks To Teachers,* we may cry because we are sad, but it is equally true that we are sad because we cry. If we want school to *feel* like a special place, there is no better way to begin than by requiring students to dress in a manner befitting the seriousness of the enterprise and the institution. I should add, teachers as well. I know of one high school in which the principal has put forward a dress code of sorts for teachers. (He has not, apparently, had the courage to propose one for the students.) For males the requirement is merely a jacket and tie. One of his teachers bitterly complained to me that such a regulation infringed upon his civil rights. And yet, this teacher will accept without complaint the same regulation when it is enforced by an elegant restaurant. His complaint and his acquiescence tell a great deal about how he values schools and how he values restaurants. Apparently, owners of elegant restaurants know more about how to create an atmosphere in a social situation than do many school principals and teachers who appear indifferent to the symbolic meaning of dress.

Of course, I do not have in mind, for students, uniforms of the type sometimes worn in parochial schools. I am referring here to some reasonable standard of dress which would mark school as a place of dignity and seriousness. And I might add that I do not believe for one moment the argument that poor people would be unable to clothe their children properly if such a code were in force. In particular, I do not believe that poor people have advanced that argument. It is an argument that middle-class education critics have made in behalf of the poor.

Another argument advanced in behalf of the poor and oppressed is that which I discussed in Chapter Nine, namely, the students' right to their own language. I have never heard this argument come from parents whose children are not competent to use Standard English. It is an argument, once again, put forward by "liberal" education critics whose children are competent in Standard English but who in some curious way wish to express their solidarity with and charity for those who are less capable. It is a case of pure condescension, and I do not think teachers should be taken in by it. Like the mode of dress, the mode of language in school ought to be relatively formal and exemplary, and therefore markedly different from the custom in less rigorous places. It is particularly important that teachers should avoid trying to win their students' affection by adopting the language of youth. Such teachers frequently win only the contempt of their students who sense that there ought to be a difference between the language of teachers and the language of students; that is to say, the world of adults and the world of children.

In this connection, it is worth saying that the modern conception of childhood is a product of the sixteenth century, as Philippe Ariès has documented in his *Centuries of Childhood*. Prior to that century, children as young as six and seven were treated in all important respects as if they were adults. Their language, their dress, their legal status, their responsibilities, their labor, were much the same as those of adults. For complex reasons, some of which concern the development of printing, the spread of literacy, and the need for early formal education, the concept of childhood as an identifiable stage in human growth began to develop in the sixteenth century and has continued into our own times. The modern conception of school and, in particular, of a classroom are accommodations to the idea that there are important distinctions to be made between childhood and adulthood. However, with the emergence of electronic media of communication, a reversal of this trend seems to be taking place. In a culture in which the distribution of information is almost wholly undifferentiated, age categories begin to disappear. Television, all by itself, may bring an end to childhood. In truth, there is no such thing as "children's programming," at least not for children over the age of eight or nine. Everyone sees and hears the same thing. The media eliminate secrets. As a consequence legal distinctions begin to appear arbitrary, as do distinctions in dress, language, styles of entertainment, games, eating habits, etc. We have already reached a point where the crimes of youth are indistinguishable from those of adults, and we may soon reach a point where the punishments will be the same. Oddly, some of our most advanced social critics have come out in favor of laws that would eliminate most of the distinctions between child and adult in the area of civil rights. This they do in the interests of "liberating" children. The effect would be to help push us back rapidly to the fifteenth century, when children were as liberated as everyone else, and just as unprotected.

I raise this point because the school is one of our few remaining institutions based on firm distinctions between childhood and adulthood, and a theory of a conserving education would include the (eighteenth and nineteenth centuries) wish that such distinctions be maintained. The school, unlike the media, is based on the assumption that adults have something of value to teach the young, and that there are differences between the behavior of adults and the behavior of children. That is why it is necessary for teachers to avoid emulating in dress and speech the style of the young. It is also why the school ought properly to be a place for what we might call "manners education": The adults in school ought to be concerned with teaching youth a standard of civilized interaction.

Again, those who are inclined to regard this as superficial may be underestimating the biases of media such as television, radio, and recorder, which teach with as much power as parental teaching how one is to conduct oneself in public. In particular, with the possible exception of movies, which still require a communal setting, the media favor an individualized and egocentric response to information. In a general sense the media "unprepare" the young for behavior in groups. A young man who goes through the day with a radio affixed to his ear is not only listening to the sound of a different drummer. He is learning to be indifferent to any shared sound. A young woman who can turn off a television program which does not suit her needs at the moment is learning impatience with any stimulus that is not responsive to her interests.

But school is not a radio station or a television program. It is a social situation requiring the subordination of one's own impulses and interests to those of the group. In a word, manners. As a rule, elementary school teachers will exert considerable effort in teaching manners. I believe they refer to this effort as "socializing the child." But it is astonishing how precipitously this effort is diminished at higher levels. It is certainly neglected in the high schools, and where it is not, there is usually an excessive concern for "bad habits," such as smoking, drinking, and, in some nineteenth-century schools, swearing. But as William James noted, our virtues are as habitual as our vices. Where is the attention given to the "Good morning" habit, to the "I beg your pardon" habit, to the "Please forgive the interruption" habit?

I hesitate to offer the following example since you will think me, for giving it, hopelessly romantic, but the most civilized high school class I have ever seen was one in which both students and teacher said good morning to each other (because the teacher always said it to his students) and in which the students actually stood up when they had something to say. The teacher, moreover, thanked each student for any contribution made to the class, did not sit with his feet on the desk, and did not interrupt a student unless he had asked permission to do so. The students, in turn, did not interrupt each other, or chew gum, or read comic books when they were bored. To avoid being a burden to others when one is bored is the essence of civilized behavior.

Of this teacher I might also say that he made no attempt to entertain his students or model his classroom along the lines of a TV program. He was concerned not only to teach his students manners but to teach them how to attend in a classroom, which is partly a matter of manners but is also necessary to their intellectual development. One of the more serious difficulties teachers now face in the classroom results from the fact that their students have media-shortened attention spans and have become accustomed, also through intense media exposure, to novelty, variety, and entertainment. Some teachers have made desperate attempts to keep their students "tuned in" by fashioning their classes along the lines of *Sesame Street* or *The Tonight Show.* They tell jokes. They change the pace. They show films, play records, and avoid any lecture or discussion that would take more than eight minutes. They avoid *anything* that would take more than eight minutes. Although its motivation is understandable, this is the worst possible thing they can do because it is what their students least need. However difficult it may be, the teacher must try to achieve student attention and even enthusiasm through the attraction of ideas, not razzmatazz. Those who think I am speaking here in favor of "dull" classes may themselves, through media exposure, have lost an understanding of the potential for excitement contained in an idea. The media (one prays) are not so powerful that they can obliterate in the young, particularly in the adolescent, what James referred to as a "theoretic instinct": a need to know reasons, causes, abstract conceptions. Such an "instinct" can be seen in its earliest stages in what he calls the "sporadic metaphysical inquiries of children as to who made God, and why they have five fingers." But it takes a more compelling and sustained form in adolescence, and may certainly be developed by teachers if they are willing to stand fast and resist the seductions of our media environment.

I trust that the reader is not misled by what I have been saying. As I see it, there is nothing in any of the above that leads to the conclusion that I favor a classroom that is authoritarian or coldhearted, or dominated by a teacher insensitive to students and how they learn. So far I have been discussing ideas by which the environment of school may be made more serious, dignified, and orderly. I do not imagine I have said anything original. I want merely to affirm the importance of the classroom as a special place, aloof from the biases of the media; a place in which the uses of the intellect are given prominence in a setting of elevated language, civilized manners, and respect for social symbols.

On the issue of how teachers might facilitate the learning of subjects, I would reaffirm many of the assumptions expressed in *Teaching as a Subversive Activity*. I still believe, for example, that good learners have confidence in their ability to learn, tend to enjoy solving problems, prefer to rely on their own judgments, are respectful of facts, abjure fast answers, and are not fearful of being wrong. And I believe that teachers can and ought to design their methods of teaching in such ways as to promote all of these characteristics. For example I would argue, even more so today than in 1967, that the principal methodological blunder committed by most teachers is that they place too great an emphasis on students' being right, and do not sufficiently appreciate the role of error in learning. As a consequence, students are made to fear being wrong, and so enduring is this fear that some of them spend much of their lives trying to protect their beliefs from criticism. Henry Perkinson in *The Possibilities of Error,* a book I would strongly recommend to every teacher, calls this attitude "justificationism," and places much of the blame for it on our methods of teaching.[1] A justificationist attitude directs learners to justify, prove, defend, and insist upon what they believe, since being "correct" is rather more than an intellectual imperative. It is a psychological imperative. Being correct, we have been taught, is the best way to avoid humiliation and other forms of punishment. Perkinson proposes that a "fallibilist" attitude is much more appropriate because it is more intellectually and psychologically sound. The fallibilist proceeds from the assumption that all human beings are fallible, especially in their ideas. Thus, the fallibilists assume that their own ideas contain errors and can be improved through criticism. Energies are devoted not to justifying one's beliefs but to investigating them in the certainty that they contain errors and in the hope of eliminating some of them. As it happens, Henry Perkinson is a colleague of mine, and I have seen him teach many times. I can report that he not only practices what he preaches but that what he preaches *can* be practiced. It is astonishing to see how students can shed some of the fear, lodged deep within them, of being wrong, when they find themselves with a teacher who does not demand that they be right but asks only that they join him in a search for error—his as well as their own. I fancy that I myself have learned something about a fallibilist orientation and, if I may say it, would offer this book as an illustration of its meaning to me.

What is especially significant about a fallibilist approach is that it is more than a method of learning. It is very close to a method of living. I know of no better way of defining "mental health" than to say it is the ability to scrutinize one's own beliefs with detachment and honesty, toward the aim of exorcising error and reducing mistakes.

Another example of a "methodological" bias of the classroom that I believe needs to be eliminated is the "fast answer" syndrome. It has been said, notably by Benjamin Bloom, that a normal child can learn anything, given enough time in which to do it. Frankly, I do not know if this is true, and I doubt if Bloom does either. But I think it reasonable to say that it is a serious mistake to connect learning so directly to speed of learning, or at least to speed of answering. So many aspects of the classroom, from teacher-student dialogue to formal tests, put a premium on being able to think fast that, at times, some classrooms begin to resemble a TV game show. I believe I understand where the obsession with speed comes from (the media, again) but I do not see anything of value accomplished by it. What I mostly see is that students are rewarded for being glib and discouraged from being thoughtful.

I still retain my belief that the "inquiry method" is a useful and in some respects an essential idea in the development of intelligence. The simplest definition of the inquiry method is that it is a process of learning in which the student assumes a heavy burden in solving intellectual problems. This requires that students learn how to ask questions, how to collect data, and how to form generalizations of a nontrivial nature. In the context of a serious subject matter and under the guidance of a skillful teacher, there is no better way for students to learn about the meaning of scholarship. But for two reasons I am somewhat less enthusiastic than I once was about recommending it. The first is that too many teachers have used the inquiry method as an excuse to bypass the teaching of any systematic content. From what I have written in the last few chapters, you will know that I believe the schools ought to confront students with important content— ideas, theories, histories, connections, questions. It is, from my point of view, unacceptable in our present situation to have students learn inquiry skills without having them applied to important subjects.

A second reason for my dampened enthusiasm is that in the hands of a teacher of technocrat mentality, the inquiry method loses its spirit and is reduced to a set of mechanical procedures. There is, in fact, no method of teaching which cannot be distorted, made into busy work or worse, when it is technicalized, which is why I believe now, as I did years ago, that all methods texts are in essence nonsense. There is no escaping the fact that the principal "method" of any classroom is the personality and the knowledge of the teacher, which is to say, teaching is an art. There are as many methods of good teaching as there are ways by which teachers communicate a love of learning, a respect for facts, a fascination for an idea. There is no such thing as an effective method in the custody of a defective teacher. I have never known a bad teacher who could be improved by a good method. And I have never known a good teacher who needed one. One can, of course, argue (as I have) that teachers must not ignore the role of error in learning, must not equate speed with understanding, must allow their students freedom to question and to explore, etc. But these are not methods. They are cliches. In the end all good teaching is made up of such cliches.

12

Evaluation

Some years ago, when I thought somewhat differently about the issues discussed in this book, I wrote an education fable. The fable was about a city which had fallen on hard times. Ugliness, decay, and conflict were everywhere. In desperation, the city's leaders decided to use the children of the city to save the situation. They scrapped the curriculum, pulled the children out of school, and organized them into teams. The idea was to have the children clean the streets, deliver the mail, repair broken buildings, plant trees and flowers, direct traffic, staff Day Care centers, and even give public concerts and plays. In my fable everything worked beautifully, as we may be permitted to have them do in fables. Ugliness disappeared, decay was halted, conflict turned to harmony. The fable was published in *The New York Times Magazine,* not once but twice, and drew an interested reaction from city dwellers and educators in many parts of the country.[1]

Now, there were many things wrong with the fable, among them that it could easily be read as an Illichian exercise in utopianism, for which, I fear, there is a large and sympathetic audience. Of course, I had not meant it to be read that way but rather as a metaphor whose purpose was to loosen our thinking about the uses of education. Nonetheless, I should have realized that many good people would interpret it as a literal proposal for education reform. Senator S. I. Hayakawa, for example, described it approvingly to his colleagues in the United States Senate, and then used the occasion to attack labor unions which, he felt, could be expected to oppose such a plan at every point. But what astonished me most were those who wrote to me in the following vein: "Your proposal is unrealistic because it contains no procedures by which we could *evaluate* the students. How would we know if they were directing traffic competently? Or cleaning the streets adequately? Or planting flowers properly? Until that problem is solved, your proposal cannot become a reality." I was, accordingly, urged to do a follow-up article specifying the evaluation procedures to be used.

Putting aside the obvious reply that our children could hardly do very much worse than we have been able to manage, I would have thought evaluation to be the *last* of the problems my fable posed, even to one who was concerned to convert the idea to reality. But of course I underestimated the power of the Technical Thesis, for one of its axioms is that evaluation procedures take precedence over ideas; this being followed closely by the axiom that methods of producing precise and quantified evaluations take precedence over all other methods.

The subject of this chapter is evaluation. But before proceeding, I should like to make it clear that I have no arguments in principle against evaluation. I believe it to be an inevitable, necessary, and natural part of all human communication. Sometimes it is called "feedback," sometimes "grades," sometimes "audience response," sometimes "criticism." But whatever it is called, there is no denying that when A does something, B will have an opinion about how well it has been done, and without such opinions we would find it quite impossible to improve ourselves. In school, these opinions must of necessity have some formal mode of expression, as well as informal. Against this there can be no complaint. I do however have some arguments against the way evaluations are in fact handled in school. In this chapter I should like to present these arguments, and suggest some ways by which the processes of evaluation may be improved. It is not my intention to be very thorough. The subject of evaluation is large and complex, and I do not have objections to or, indeed, opinions about every aspect of it. I shall address only that which seems to me most in want of improvement.

The first argument consists of the commonsense view that what is to be evaluated, and how, must be decided *after* we determine what is worth doing. In fact, the opposite is frequently the case in schools. For example, when a standardized reading test is used, we can always be sure that it is the test itself that has determined what shall be evaluated. A standardized test is by definition impersonal and only by rare coincidence evaluates what a particular teacher or parent might be interested in knowing. In saying this, I do not mean that teachers and parents aren't interested in evaluating the reading abilities of their children. In a general way, test makers, being business people, try to respond to their customers' needs. But reading is an exceedingly complex process, and there are multiple dimensions to the evaluation of reading behavior. Who is to decide which of these dimensions is worth evaluating?

For example, I have never thought it particularly revealing to discover, as many reading tests will do, if a student can pick out an appropriate title for a paragraph. Neither do I want to know very much if a student can identify the antonym of some particular word. I know people who can do these things quite well but who are, in my opinion, virtual illiterates. I might hasten to say that I do not regard such skills as picking out titles and identifying antonyms as meaningless. I am simply objecting to their being used to form an important part of a definition of reading abilities. And who has decided to employ this definition? Test makers, not teachers. In fact, very few teachers I have known would select these skills as a basis for determining literacy.

For my own part, and I am far from alone in this, I would want to know some quite different things. For example, confronted by a text of any kind or complexity, a reader must make some assessment of its purpose. I would have thought that a text which has as its title "An Education Fable" and begins with the words "Once upon a time . . ." would have sufficiently indicated that the writer is not going to offer a curriculum guide for the schools. But there are many readers who have the greatest difficulty in discerning tone in language, and this will always be an obstacle to their ability to assess purpose. Therefore, how well a reader can determine tone and purpose seems to me a vital question, one which is rarely addressed by a reading test.

I am also interested in knowing how well a reader can assess the "truth" content of a passage, provided that the purpose of the text invites that question. Of course, if the purpose of a text is to tell a joke or a fable, the question of the truth of the sentences is not relevant. I came across a marvelous example of this sort of misreading during the preparation of my last book, which was about language. In the context of a discussion of the "herd instinct" which leads people to chant slogans such as "Heil Hitler," I had permitted myself a small joke. As a graduate of Columbia University, I said that sloganeering and chanting at football games ("Go Lions!") were probably acceptable forms of behavior, especially if Columbia were on Michigan State's three-yard line, and a touchdown would result in the upset of the century. A copy editor of uncommon devotion was checking the manuscript for spelling and punctuation errors, and in due course came upon this sentence. In the interests of "truth," he crossed out Michigan State and substituted Dartmouth because, he noted in the margin, Columbia does not play Michigan State. But then Columbia never has much difficulty in beating Dartmouth, which fact rather takes the point, such as it was, out of my joke.

Nonetheless, there are many kinds of texts in which accuracy of the facts is of overriding importance. How does a reader proceed in making a judgment about the question of truth? What are the strategies he or she uses in order to assign a probability rating to the alleged facts that are cited? Or does the reader have no such strategies? Does he or she simply believe everything, or disbelieve everything? If either of these is the case, I think it fair to say that such a reader has a serious problem. An equally serious problem would be an inability to distinguish between what has been put forward as a "fact" and what is offered as an "opinion." And no less serious would be an inability to grasp the point of view of the writer, or his bias, or his assumptions, or his rhetorical strategies, none of which is ever revealed by a standardized reading test.

For some curious reason, the processes of interpretation to which I am here referring are frequently categorized as "critical reading skills," and are separated from what is called "comprehension." This is a distinction encouraged by test makers, if not created by them, but in any case it is a distinction not entirely accepted by many teachers. From my own point of view, it is hard to understand how the distinction can be maintained by any educator, for even if one wishes to define "comprehension" as the capacity to produce a simple paraphrase of a text, the purpose, tone, point of view, level of abstraction, degree of credibility, etc., of the text would be part of the problem. Unless, of course, these were arbitrarily ruled out of consideration by a peculiar sort of test, in which case we would not be testing what I and many others call "reading abilities."

I have raised this issue to make several related points. The first is that a standardized test represents an educational thesis. It is in no sense a neutral evaluation. It does not just measure. It tells us what to measure. When we expose our students to such a test, we are accepting, whether we like it or not, the test maker's conception of reading abilities, of intelligence, of cultural knowledge, or whatever.

A second point is that the test maker's thesis will be expressed as much through the form of the test as through its content. This is the case with all tests but special problems arise when the test makers have no direct contact with those whom they are testing. They are then almost certain to design tests that are artificial and arbitrary. For example, it is obvious that if I want to know how well students can paraphrase a text, the best way to do it is to ask them to write or speak the paraphrase. Certainly, if I want to know how well students can grasp the purpose or tone or credibility or bias of a text, I *must* ask them to say or write something about the text. But standardized tests never take this commonsense approach, for if students were to speak or write about a text, their answers would be complex and difficult to evaluate. The test would take time, and much would depend on the teacher's ability to assess the student's response. Thus, the test would become "unstandardized." What one wants to do in making up a standardized test is to save time, reduce complexity, eliminate teacher judgment. As a consequence, the *form* of such a test must result in a distorted definition of whatever it is one is testing for.

It may come as a surprise to some but there are many ways to give reading tests. For example, in trying to determine some of the problems students have in reading, I have tried the following: I have presented students with a text that is essentially a report of an event. I have then asked them to choose some statement that they believe has high credibility and one that has low credibility, and then to indicate the reasons for their judgment. Or, I have asked students to make a list of statements that are *not* included in the text but which readers might conjecture are being concealed from them (for what a writer does not say is sometimes as important as what he does). Or, to give an example which I have used many times with young students both to evaluate their ability to grasp tone and to teach them something about it: I have provided students with two wedding invitations. The first says, "Mr. and Mrs. Irving Freebish request the honor of your presence, on September 7, 1980, at the wedding of their daughter, Katherine." The second says, "Irving and me would like you to be there (Sept. 7) when Kathy gets hitched." The questions that follow run along these lines: At what sort of place do you think each of these weddings is likely to occur? What sort of food would you expect to be served at each of these weddings? What sort of clothing do you think will be worn? What sort of gift would you be inclined to give?

What I am trying to say is that these problems, these questions, and the forms of response they require *constitute a reading test.* They may also be used as instruments for teaching reading. But what is astonishing to me is that so many people, including teachers, will not think of these problems as representing a real reading test. Why? I believe the answer is that the *form* of standardized reading tests has become completely accepted as *the method* of evaluating reading. But a reading test does not have to consist of short answers of the type that says choose A,B,C, or D. It does not have to say, "You have twenty minutes to complete this test." It does not have to produce a score, such as 7.3. Tests of this type do not, in my opinion, have important educational meaning. They are given because they are convenient and because they reflect the information bias of our culture.

After all, a citizenry that will not fall down from laughing at a beauty contest which rates poise as a 4.236 can be expected to be duly serious about a reading test that says, You are a 7.3. In other words, as a technicalized people, we want tests which do not require us to listen to what children have to say, or to read what they have written. We want tests that can be given in a day or two to everybody. We want tests that do not rely on human judgment. And we want numbers.

Well, this is what we have got, which might have been bearable but for one thing: Once a standardized test has defined what we shall know, and specified how we shall know it, and has ruled out all other possibilities, that definition tends to become the *content* of much of our teaching. The situation develops something like this: Suppose many schools around the country took my education fable literally and decided to put its suggestions into practice. We would discover almost immediately that each school would do it somewhat differently, emphasizing certain things, discarding others, adding still others. Much would depend on the professional judgment of teachers, the needs of the community, the wishes of the parents. Such diversity is exactly what we would want. I certainly would want it if educators took seriously the proposals made in this book. But now imagine that the test makers entered the picture, claiming that there is too much variation, that standards of evaluation are not uniform and that the nation needs to know how well schools are doing their job. They would then produce a series of tests designed to give us quantified information about ourselves. In designing the tests they would have to define what behaviors are important in, let us say, directing traffic (which, you will recall, is one of the things the children must do in my fable). And let us imagine that they determined that the behavior that best lends itself to quantification is how many traffic tickets are given out. At that point, competence in directing traffic would come to mean exactly the same thing as a certain number of traffic tickets given out. (If twenty tickets a week were the average given by tenth graders, any tenth grade student giving less would be below grade level, and how much below could be stated in precise mathematical terms.) Now comes the danger point: Even teachers who did not agree with this definition of competence would, nonetheless, begin to orient their students toward giving out tickets and neglect anything else that might be relevant to directing traffic. Parents, of course, would expect teachers to emphasize the giving of tickets even if they, too, thought the whole business absurd. In short, it is understandable and inevitable that teachers and parents will want their children to score well on standardized tests—*whether the tests measure things of significance or not.* Accordingly, there is always a tendency to prepare children for tests by teaching what the tests emphasize. In this way the curriculum moves out of the control of teachers and parents, and into the hands of test makers.

If I intended this book to be an education fable, I would argue here that standardized tests of all types be eliminated from the schools. Ideally, I should like to see them barred in perpetuity from educational contexts. The presence of these tests prevents us from determining in a rational way what is worth doing; and the tests provide us with distorted definitions of educational concepts such as reading abilities, intelligence, and knowledge. Moreover, I do not believe it is necessary for the "nation" to know how schools are doing, which is a major argument for using them. The "nation," in my opinion, already knows more than it should about the affairs of its citizens. And, in any case, we can assume that parents and teachers want the best for their children and that their efforts do not need to be monitored by super-agencies. Besides, even if one takes the position that the "nation" *does* need to know how schools are doing, who will make the decision as to what we ought to test *for?* Are there any standardized tests that will tell us, for example, how well our children understand the history and philosophy of science? Are there any standardized tests that tell us how well our children understand the impact of media on culture? Why not? Who has decided that the "nation" does not need to know these things about our children but does need to know how well they are doing in mathematics?

But this book is not intended to be a fable, and my questions are therefore somewhat idle. The test-making enterprise is big business and there is no realistic hope of eliminating standardized tests from the school picture. Although we may be encouraged by the opposition to national testing programs by teacher organizations (who fear that test results will be used unfairly to judge teacher competence), the fact is that impersonal testing is here to stay. There are simply too many institutions, including colleges and professional schools, that rely on standardized tests, and we cannot expect much diminution in their use. But it is possible to be judicious in using such testing procedures, and the following list of questions is offered in the hope of assisting educators in their selection of standardized tests:

1. Exactly what does the test purport to measure?

2. What, in actual fact, does it measure?

3. What are its basic definitions of the skills, attitudes, or understandings it claims to measure?

4. How consistent are these definitions with those of the teachers in the school?

5. What does the test *not* measure that, in the opinion of teachers, ought to be evaluated?

6. What does the test force a school to teach that, in the opinion of teachers, is not worthwhile?

7. What behaviors and ways of thinking does the *form* of the test promote? Do teachers regard these as worthwhile?

8. What supplementary tests will be required in order to give a fuller account of the student's abilities?

9. To what extent does the test measure speed of response? Is speed a positive or negative factor in assessing the student's ability?

10. To what extent can the test be used as a teaching instrument?

11. What are the main uses of the results of the test? To help students? To punish students? To advance the careers of politicians? To undermine confidence in teachers?

I fear that, to this point, I have given the impression that the only problems with evaluation are those generated by standardized tests. But this is surely not so. A test does not have to be designed by the Educational Testing Service or Harcourt Brace in order to be stupid, distorted, or hypocritical. As a teacher of more than twenty years' service, I have given my share of awful tests, without any assistance from the businessmen in Princeton or New York. My main difficulty is hypocrisy, although it stems, I believe, more from a want of ingenuity than a want of sincerity. I know what I wish my students to learn, but I cannot always invent ways to assess these learnings. As a consequence, I have found myself giving tests that evaluate something else, then pretending I have measured what I thought important. I daresay that most teachers have difficulties of this sort, and I have nothing to recommend as a corrective except eternal vigilance. For example, I think it perfectly legitimate to give a short-answer test which tries to determine if students have knowledge in a certain area. But one must avoid believing that such a test tells you very much beyond the limits of both the form and content of the particular questions that have been asked. Everyone has had the experience of submitting to a short-answer test which did not ask about those things one knew most thoroughly. In other words, formal tests, while sometimes useful, can be a snare and a delusion. What one needs to guard against is the tendency of a test to take over the functions of human judgment and to establish itself as *the method* of student assessment. There are, for example, dozens of informal observations a teacher can make that will tell more about a student than any formal test ever produced. I should say that after two months of classes, a good teacher does not require a formal test to know what deficiencies a student has. Evaluation is not something that happens on Friday. Every class is a test. Every interaction is a test. Every response is a test.

That is to say, they are if the teacher is skillful in observing behavior and in diagnosing learning deficiencies. But sad to say, many teachers are not adept at either, and particularly lack both experience and knowledge in diagnosing learning problems. This is probably why (at least in part) our grading system takes the form that it does. Most teachers can tell if one student is better than another in a particular skill or subject. In general, teachers do not have great difficulty in assigning a grade which reflects a student's performance relative to that of other students. But a grade is a summation, not really an evaluation—and still less a diagnosis. The main problem with the grading system is not that we use numbers or letters, but that our numbers and letters are rarely accompanied by intelligible descriptions and explanations of student weaknesses.

If our present system of student evaluation were used by the medical profession, doctors would give us grades—A, B, C, D, F—based on their judgment of our health relative to that of others, and then send us packing. Of course, doctors do "grade" us when they make such statements as "Well, I think you're going to be all right" (B+ ?) or "I'm afraid you're not well" (C− ?). But doctors are required to go beyond this. Their summary statements are only the beginning of their evaluations. We expect them to tell us what, specifically, we need to do in order to get better, and we may even expect them to indicate the reasons why we have become sick in the first place. Without a diagnosis and a prescription, the doctor's judgment would be virtually useless, except perhaps to companies that sell life insurance. But this is exactly the situation in our schools at the present time. There are summary statements, but no diagnosis and no prescription. The summary statements—"She is an A−" or "He is a seventy-two"—are useful to colleges and professional schools, but they do not tell anyone, including the learner, what the problems are and how they might be overcome.

This is not an easy situation to correct. One of its several causes, I believe, lies in the fact that the study of learning is very far from being a science. For all of its pretensions, educational psychology cannot tell us very much about why or how people learn, not even why or how people do not learn. It sometimes seems to me that most educational psychologists are not even interested in the question. But this is not a matter we can do much about, except to wish Jean Piaget the best of luck and hope that his researches will eventually establish the basis of a useful discipline.

But teachers do not have to wait upon that happy outcome before improving their methods of student assessment. What would be required of them is a shift in their thinking about remediation. As things stand now, most teachers do not pay much attention to learning difficulties except when a student falls far behind others in learning whatever the teacher requires. If enough students fall behind, remedial classes are established where all the "reluctant" or "slow" learners may be dealt with at the same time. But the point I wish to make is that *all learning is remedial.* If I may dare to contradict Professor Dewey's best-known aphorism, we do not learn by doing; we learn by *not* doing. By trial and error. By making mistakes, correcting them, making more mistakes, correcting them, and so on. The "and so on" is important here, because the process of making mistakes has no end. There is no one who learns how to write or read or calculate or think once and for all. To the end of his life Carl Sandburg, for example, was still struggling, as he himself has told us, to learn the uses of nouns and verbs. As for reading, if the work of I. A. Richards has taught us anything, it is that no one, not even Richards himself, knows how to read. To be sure, some readers make fewer mistakes than others. But there is no one who reaches a point where remediation is not necessary.

Every student in a classroom, therefore, has learning difficulties—the A students as well as the F. If teachers grasped this idea, they would inevitably pay more attention to mistakes and errors than they do at present, and would be closer to a professional position in advising students about how to improve themselves. In fact I believe it would be entirely possible to teach any course—not only English or math, but history, economics, biology, and physics—as a study in mistaken beliefs, debilitating prejudices, and inadequate skills. This is perhaps what the old-line progressives had in mind when they instructed us to "start where the student is." That is sound advice, because where the students "are" is where their errors are. What a student does not know, and cannot do, is where education begins.

But fortunately for educators, student ignorance and ineptness are neither random nor unique. Teachers who have paid close attention can predict in advance of meeting a class what sorts of mistakes will be made by students when they confront a particular question, concept, text, or assignment. Mistakes are a patterned form of human behavior, and some of the best work that has been done in what *I* would call educational psychology (but "educational psychologists" wouldn't) has had "mistakes" as its focus. I refer, for example, to I. A. Richards's *Practical Criticism,* in which he identifies and classifies the errors readers make in comprehending poetry. Or S. I. Hayakawa's *Language in Thought and Action,* in which he discusses the common "thinking" errors made by people in a wide spectrum of contexts. Or Mina Shaughnessy's recent *Errors and Expectations,* in which she analyzes the patterns of errors made by college students when writing. Even the work of Piaget himself may be seen as studies in what children cannot do, and why.

But there do not exist, so far as I know, studies and texts on the subject of mistakes in learning biology, or mistakes in learning history, or mistakes in learning art, or mistakes in learning economics, etc. In their absence most teachers will have to do such studies on their own—and in fact, some have. For there are teachers who, because they have paid close attention to mistakes, can anticipate patterns of error, prepare correctives for them, and provide students with intelligible descriptions of their weaknesses.

In this connection it remains for me to say that the principal objection I have to the grouping of students—for example, into "smart" (the Bluebirds), "average" (the Starlings), and "dumb" (the Robins)—is that such a procedure assumes that the Robins have learning difficulties while the Bluebirds do not. If this piece of nonsense were eliminated from our thinking, much of the offensiveness of homogeneous grouping would disappear. That is to say, I do believe in "inability grouping," provided that teachers are capable of specifying the nature of the "inabilities." In saying this, I do not wish to ally myself with those of a strict behaviorist outlook, especially those who prattle about "behavioral objectives." Obviously, teachers need to know how to observe behavior and to interpret its meaning; they need to know what sorts of things students cannot do, and how to develop strategies to help them overcome their deficiencies. And they need to know how much they and their students are accomplishing. But we must not make too much of evaluation. As I remarked earlier, we must certainly avoid allowing our ideas about education to be controlled by our technical capacity to measure what we do. It shall be a sad day for all of us when we teach only those things for which there are easily discernible behavioral outcomes. In that case, we will have given up trying to have our students know things and believe things. We will have given up talking about most of the things that distinguish human education from animal training.

In the end education is an act of faith in the power of ideas to have consequences unforeseen and unmeasurable. Therefore, we must do with our children what seems rational and decent and useful to do. What I have proposed in this book, for example, seems all of those things to me. As a consequence, I shall not conclude by saying "Or vice versa," for I am deeply convinced that what I have said in these pages will help to prepare our children for an amiable meeting with their future. Of course, I should not be surprised if on another occasion, with me or our culture vastly changed, I shall see things differently. But at the moment, I shall stand with this.

Notes

Chapter 1

1. For a succinct expression of Riesman's views on this idea, I would urge you to read his essay "Values in Context," in *Individualism Reconsidered,* The Free Press, 1954. For a fuller discussion, see his *Constraint and Variety in American Education,* Anchor Books, 1958.

2. To quote Cremin directly: "[Riesman's] suggestion has a good deal of merit; after all, one definition of an intellectual is a man who thinks otherwise. But Riesman's ideal could easily become as inflexible as Dewey's concern for bringing the schools closer to life." *The Genius of American Education,* Vintage Books, 1965, p. 22.

3. See Lasch's *Haven in a Heartless World: The Family Besieged,* Basic Books, 1977.

Chapter 2

1. See Ong's *The Presence of the Word*, Yale University Press, 1967, particularly Chapter Two, "Transformations of the Word," from which (p. 34) his quotation in the text was taken.

2. Immediately before the sentence I have quoted, Socrates said: "A terrible thing about writing, Phaedrus, is this, and here, in truth, it is like painting. I mean, the creations of the painter stand like living creatures, but if you ask them anything, they maintain a solemn silence. And so it is with writings; you might think they spoke as if they had intelligence, but if you put a question with a wish for information on a point in what is said, there is one, one only, invariable reply."

3. The point of view I have taken in my discussion of Plato is borrowed entirely from Eric Havelock, whose books *Preface to Plato, Prologue to Literacy,* and *Origins of Western Literacy* I strongly recommend. That there are other interpretations of Plato's banishment of poets goes without saying.

Chapter 4

1. I mean these remarks about the hemispheres of the brain (as well as those that follow) to be taken only half seriously. In the first place, you will notice that my comments have a distinct Lamarckian flavor to them. In the second, I know very little about neurology and brain research. I include these speculations because I find them both plausible and interesting, but I vow, here and now, to make no further comments about the structure of the brain until such time as I have a medical degree, with a specialty in brain research.

2. See Julian Jaynes's *The Origin of Consciousness in the Breakdown of the Bicameral Mind,* Houghton Mifflin, 1976. In con-

trast to me, Jaynes knows a great deal about the structure of the brain and has written the most fascinating book on the subject of consciousness I have ever read. If you are not put off by the book's discouraging title, you will enjoy a delightful intellectual adventure.

3. See the front page of *The New York Times,* February 27, 1978.

4. McLuhan has made several remarks conveying this idea. The one quoted here was taken from *Dreadnaught Broadside,* an unusual series of pamphletlike publications produced by students at the University of Toronto.

5. For an interesting discussion of this idea see José Ortega y Gasset's *The Revolt of the Masses,* W. W. Norton, 1932, particularly Chapter 13, where, among other things, he notes the astonishing growth in police departments throughout the "civilized" world.

6. For a well-developed argument on this point see Joshua Meyrowitz's *No Sense of Place: A Theory on the Impact of Electronic Media on Social Structure and Behavior,* unpublished doctoral dissertation, New York University, 1978.

7. This quotation is found in *Understanding Media,* McGraw-Hill, 1965, p. 305. Several others similar to it may be found throughout *Understanding Media.*

Chapter 5

1. To prove to yourself that I have not made this up, you may write to HAGOTH Corporation, 85 N.W. Alder Place, Dept. C, Issaquah, Washington, 98027.

2. The best work that has been done in making explicit, i.e., visible, the rules of such situations can be found in the books of Erving Goffman of the University of Pennsylvania, particularly his *Behavior in Public Places,* Free Press of Glencoe, 1963.

3. Beyond doubt the world's authority on technicalization is Jacques Ellul. See his book *The Technological Society,* Vintage Books, 1964.

4. See Christine Nystrom's "Immediate Man," *Et cetera,* Spring 1977.

5. See Joseph Weizenbaum's *Computer Power and Human Reason,* W. H. Freeman, 1976, p. 203.

Chapter 6

1. See Wendell Johnson's *People in Quandaries,* Harper & Brothers, 1946.

2. In saying this, I do not mean that all such programs ought to be eliminated. For example, there may be compelling reasons for special programs for the physically handicapped. I am speaking here against the assumption that the existence of differences among students requires a special program as a response.

Chapter 7

1. See *The New York Times,* June 17, 1978.

2. See *Science News,* July 8, 1978.

3. Among several books that may be used by teachers are Catherine Minteer's *Words and What They Do to You,* S. I. Hayakawa's *Language in Thought and Action,* and Wendell Johnson's *Your Most Enchanted Listener.* For a full listing of such books write to the International Society for General Semantics, P.O. Box 2469, San Francisco, California 94126.

Chapter 8

1. See *The Encyclopedia of Educational Research,* under the heading "Grammar."

2. In order to avoid misunderstanding, I should note that Friere's work in the teaching of reading (for example, in his *Pedagogy of the Oppressed*) has a far greater political orientation than I or Ashton-Warner or Kohl have in mind. Friere's methods of teaching reading are intended to lead to a heightened political consciousness, and then to revolution. Whether one agrees with his aims or not, the point is that learning to read is not merely a technical skill.

Chapter 9

1. For the complete text of this extraordinary proclamation, write to The National Council of Teachers of English, Champaign, Illinois.

Chapter 10

1. P. 126 in *Technics and Civilization,* Harcourt, Brace & World, ·1963.

2. For an elaboration of this idea see Kenneth Boulding's *The Meaning of the Twentieth Century,* Harper Colophon Books, 1965, particularly Chapter Two.

3. Perhaps the most interesting textbook available is *City as Classroom: Understanding Language and Media,* by Marshall

McLuhan, Kathryn Hutchon, and Eric McLuhan. It is published by The Book Society of Canada Limited, in Ontario.

I can also recommend as a text Reuel Denney's *The Astonished Muse: Popular Culture in America,* The Universal Library, Grosset & Dunlap, 1964. And *The Future of Literacy,* edited by Robert Disch, Prentice-Hall, 1973. For general background I would recommend: Edmund Carpenter and Marshall McLuhan, *Explorations in Communication,* Beacon Press, 1960; Eric Havelock, *Preface to Plato,* Harvard University Press, 1963; William Kuhns, *The Post-Industrial Prophets,* Weybright and Talley, 1971; and *Human Connection and the New Media,* edited by Barry Schwartz, Prentice-Hall, 1973.

Chapter 11

1. For an elaboration of this idea, see Henry Perkinson's article on Karl Popper, fallibilism, and education, in *Et cetera,* Spring 1978.

Chapter 12

1. For those who might be interested, the fable can be found in *The School Book* (written by Charles Weingartner and me), Delacorte, 1973.

Index